Kevin Lee D.O.
707.798.7320

Offspring of God
And
Play of God

Handbook of

Offspring of God
And
Play of God

IP-IL Philosophy

A New Presentation of Higher Wisdom
With Regard to the Human Soul
In the form of a Systematic Exposition

Swami R. Vaidyanathan
(REMAJI)

Edited by IP Meera Grimes

Published by G.M.S
2313, Taos Trail
Okemos, Michigan—48864
e-mail ipmeera@yahoo.com
517-347-0321

Publisher's Cataloging-in-Publication
(Provided by Quality Books, Inc.)

Vaidyanathan, R.Swami.
    Handbook of offspring of God and play of God:IP-IL
philosophy: a new presentation of higher wisdom with
regard to the human soul in the form of systematic
exposition / Swami R. Vaidyanathan (Remaji). -- 1st ed.

p. cm.
ISBN 0-9717213-0-0
    1. Hinduism. 2. Philosophy, Indic. 3. Spiritual
life--Hinduism. 4. Spirituality. I. Title.

BL1205.V352002   294.5'4
        QBI33-278

Cover Design: Jan Stevens
Printed by Sheridan Books
Printed in the United States of America

Offering

I offer these writings to you all, the future generations of this world.

My advice is that all of you should understand the IP-IL philosophy whether you want it or not, so that when the desire for liberation arises, you will know what to do.

I do not want you to do anything or change anything. Enough, if you take these ideas in you, without resisting because they are true.

They will act and you need not. By receiving what I say with assent, your duty ends.

Remaji

Swami R. Vaidyanathan (Remaji) 1960

Remaji and Meera Grimes 1988

THE SOUL REVEALS

Excerpts from Remaji's Letters
to the Editor

I am not a person. I am the incarnation of the wisdom of scriptures. Wherever religion is truly understood and practiced I am there. Through My philosophy I am trying to reduce My (World's) suffering.

I am the thought or *sankalpa* of God that man shall suffer less and behave better. This *sankalpa* will change the world and rule the world. Now do you know who I am?

I have poured into the world the greatest, sweetest wisdom it has ever had, as a normal child-like human being.

Of the philosophy that I give to the world, God is the producer, I am the mother, and *Masquism* is the child that is produced through me. It was gifted to the world from 1950 onwards.

I live to see more and more ordinary sons of God becoming good sons of God. Only a world where more and more are good sons of God can bring about a kind, ordered, decent society. Good sons of God are my wealth. I am greedy for maximum wealth. I will not rest until all mankind have become good sons of God.

Why have I spent fifty years in thinking and writing this philosophy, and for what? It is to make man love God above all, love others as he loves himself and to treat others kindly and justly. Only a younger brother of Jesus can write the above three lines because he said it first.

Through Jesus' suffering, the world was changed. If Jesus did all that he did, but did not suffer, the world would not have changed. My suffering is necessary to change the world. I give my consent gladly.

Wherever you are, God is with you. Whatever you are that is your field of service. If you love God and serve the world, I who am with you will increase in you. Christ said, "After I am gone, the Holy Ghost will help you." It is not incorrect to think of me as the Holy Ghost that Christ referred to.

Jesus said, "Love God above all and love thy neighbor as thyself and do unto others as you would be done by." I, his younger brother, have given the philosophy for that.

I, who respect and revere Buddha first and then only other great religious personalities, however teach differently. If Buddha were to advise me regarding my teaching, he would say, "Objectification of the *maskrader* and *maskrade* (ego and life) is enough. No other practice is required. Why do you bring in *Isvara* and *Isvara Putra*? (God and the offspring of God)" But I am sure that if Buddha were alive today, he would smile with approval on my teaching.

Buddha only spoke for the eradication of suffering. I too stand only for eradication of suffering. I am a spokesman for all the promulgators of Higher Wisdom or Religion. By my teaching Buddha, Sankara, Ramanuja, Kapila, Arobindo, Jesus, Mohammed, will be RIGHTLY understood. I am not here to displace the old, but to truly interpret the old. I teach ancient wisdom in modern language.

He who incarnated as Krishna, Jesus, Ramakrishna, Vivekananda is now *maskrading* as Vaidyanathan, and He is ever with you. Learn to digest this greatest of good news. He knows the truth about his Substratum Self and the truth about the world appearance.

I am a being whose every word is worth preserving in tablets of gold. I have written hundreds of thousands of pages. I don't have the heart to destroy even a scrap of paper that I have written on. Every one of my statements, I can logically substantiate. The world sees my conviction as egoism and has shunned me. There is nothing new in this. Jesus said, "Rejoice and be exceedingly glad when men revile you and persecute you. Because this is what they do to all prophets."

A time may come when the world wearies of its present social and political adventures and enterprises, and is in a mood to turn to God wholly. At that time my writings will be of much help.

Remaji 1988

CONTENTS

VIEW OF LIFE
Right Understanding of the Five Truths
Consists of Sections P, Q, R, S, T, U, and V

Remaji was born on the 6th of February 1913, in Madras, India, the second son of Mr. and Mrs. R. N. Sharma. His parents named him Vaidyanathan, and called him Chinnamani meaning little jewel. As a child he was brought up as a musician. He was well versed in both Indian and western music and could play the violin, flute and piano. Later he became a composer. First he underwent a college education and received a B.A in 1931 from Presidency College, Madras. There he received both the Bilderbeck and Elliot Prize for the first rank in English. He was also educated as a scientist. From 1931 to 1933 he studied for his MSC where he was awarded a scholarship to do research on the acoustics of musical instruments. He completed his MSC degree in 1933. The Nobel Prize winner, Sir C. V. Raman in a certificate about his thesis wrote, "For a young Indian fresh from college, this is a remarkable achievement." This enabled Remaji to enter Cambridge University in 1934, where he spent four years as a research scholar studying nuclear physics in the Cavendish Laboratory. His professor was Lord Rutherford. There, he co-authored an article on physics with A. N. May.

One day in 1936, when he was in Cambridge, his landlady came to his room at about 8.30 PM and noticing a photograph of a young girl on his table asked him "Is this your wife?" "No, she is my sister," he answered. "You are kidding. I know you Indians marry young," she said with a smile and went away.

The word 'young' struck his mind deeply. "What is young?" he asked. At once a picture of himself when he was two years old appeared in his mind. He examined this picture, and then looked at his present body, and asked, "Who is me, that or this?" In short, he discarded step by step his own personality, and at one point went beyond. Everything vanished. A Universal Consciousness awoke in him. All this happened within a span of two minutes and what happened then was the beginning. He could no longer continue his studies. So he returned to India in 1939. After that Remaji identified himself with the whole world and worked to improve it as previously he had worked to improve himself.

He became keenly aware of the vast amount of suffering that human beings obtain in the world and he began to wonder how God who ruled over such a world could be good. Two problems confronted him: an imperfect body and a suffering world. He accepted both these challenges and became a philosopher.

Remaji's musical talent helped him to take care of his hunger and his shelter. He never cashed in on his knowledge but he gave his knowledge of music and philosophy to those wanted it and in return accepted the hospitality of the receivers.

A definite philosophy emerged in 1948 or thereabouts and for the next nearly fifteen years or so he consolidated his position, working out certain details of dissemination of his ideas to achieve the intentions that he wanted. His writings, which were exclusively oriented towards the *reduction of human suffering and world welfare*, were based on a *new view of life*. The writings, which date from 1944 to 1989, are either typed or handwritten on paper, bits of paper, or in notebooks.

The idea of writing books did not appeal to him. He wished to directly interest and teach people. He personally felt that any victory won without employing the highest methods would not be permanent. So he was not willing to sell himself or his writings for lesser prizes. Remaji had a desire to be sought out and admired by humanity before he offered his work to them but that did not happen although he taught his philosophy to hundreds of people. Being a recluse, and of a retiring nature, he was little known to the world and his ideas lay hidden in his heart and in his writings.

Remaji named his philosophy *Masquism* and he explained it in the form of nine aphorisms. They are also called the *Sutras of Masquism*. The principle of *Masquism* elucidates the constitution of the universe and humanity's place in it. It does this in such a way that love of God and love of neighbor in a historical context, follow as a natural consequence. Thus, it fulfills the demand of Nature's evolution of consciousness by requiring of human beings a new and heightened self-awareness from which a new relationship to God and the world and one's neighbor follow as a natural consequence.

The message of the *aphorisms of Masquism* is non-dualistic. According to it, the sufferer is God Himself pretending to suffer. The sufferer is self-entranced God. Later he also presented his message reconciling the teachings of non-dualism and qualified non-dualism. According to it, the sufferer is *Isvara Putra* meaning the offspring or son of God, in an entranced condition or in the condition of ignorance. He referred to it as IP-IL Philosophy. This stands for *Isvara Putra Isvara Lila Siddhanta,* which means the offspring or son of God and the play of God. Thus he has given his message or explained the same truth from two different viewpoints. They are not contradictory but rather complimentary to each other. Remaji said,

It may be wondered that I sometime speak that the true individual is really, RA, the Substratum Self or *Brahman*, and then speak of the true being as offspring or son of God or *Brahma Putra* or *Isvara Putra.* How can a person be son and father, reflection and original? My answer is this. These are conceptions through right use of which we have to attain the trance-conceptual State. Other-ness to God either as His reflection or as His son, satisfy certain realistic needs during spiritual practice or *sadhana*. The son idea makes devotion, love, service, and surrender possible. That the son is like unto the father and the reflection is like unto the original, preserves the non-dualistic truth also. So, during the practice, a wise use of son and reflection will help in the liberation from selfishness and carnality.

In addition to his work on *Masquism*, he has written many articles on several other philosophical topics like the *Bhagavad Gita, Patanjali Yoga, Bhakti, Dharma, Dhyana, Mukti, Muktan, Samskaras, Vasana Kshayam* etc. He has also written his views on education, politics, personality development, self-knowledge, the mind, nature, culture, knowledge, person, motivation, behavior enhancement, mental activity, realms of knowledge, understanding, how to live for the good of the world, and so on. There are thousands of pages of his writings.

Remaji's philosophy does not displace other teach-ings, other concepts of God, or other methods of attaining God or Self-Realization. Remaji said,

> My only interest in doing what previous religions were meant to do and failed to do for various reasons is to change wild human beings into loving, kind, gentle individuals. Humans are the only creatures that have the freedom to shape their won lives. Religions contain the best answers for how one should shape one's life in the world. I am simply stating that eternal wisdom in my own way. Your own consciousness will tell you if I am right or wrong.

He breathed his last breath at Pandori, a branch of Pingalwada, an institution for neglected old, poor and disabled people, Amritsar, Punjab, India, uncared for on the 2nd of February, 1990. The institution donated his body to help the medical students of the Lakshmi Narayan Medical Institute of Amritsar, India.

Editor's Note

The extreme suffering that I experienced in my life brought the blessing of God into my life and made me remember my beloved Guru, Remaji, for the first time after fifteen years of estrangement. This happened at the end of 1987 when I was in California with my husband and our only son. My brother Sridhar who was in Madras was kind enough to find Remaji's address for me. I wrote a letter to him in October begging for his forgiveness, but I received no reply. Again I wrote to him in November. I received a letter from him dated the 26th of November 1987. Through that letter I learned that he had had an accident on June 4th, in which he had fallen from his bicycle and broken his thighbone. He had been in the hospital for several months and had almost come to the end of his physical life.

Thereafter until November of 1989 Remaji started writing letters to me regularly, instructing, refreshing, and perfecting my understanding of his teachings. I received several hundreds of pages of correspondence from him during those two years. I also visited him at Patiala, Punjab, India, in mid 1988 and reconciled with him. He left his physical body in 1990. In his will he bequeathed all of his writings and belongings to me.

In 1960, Remaji was looking for a deserving student to teach his musical compositions to, especially the music that he had set to Hindustani bhajans like Mirabai, Surdas, and others. He expressed this wish to a friend, Mr. K. S. Ayer, who also happened to be our family friend. Mr. and Mrs. Ayer recommended me to Remaji and he told my mother, Neela Balasubramaniam, about this. My parents thought it was a blessing to me. That is how I came into contact with Remaji. At the time, I was about seventeen years old and I was already a performing artist in the field of Harikatha or spiritual story telling. I was also a classical dance performer of Bharatanatyam and a vocalist. I became Remaji's music student and learned hundreds of bhajans from him. Day and night I studied under him in 'Gurukulavasa' style for about twelve years. Apart from teaching me bhajans, Remaji perfected my Carnatic and Hindustani music singing and he also introduced me to western music. He enhanced my rendering of *Harikatha* and later he taught me his philosophy and other Indian philosophical systems. I left him in the beginning of 1972.

Due to various reasons I have been unable to publish any of Remaji's writings for all of these years. This handbook will be the first publication of his work. It has been prepared primarily from his letters to me of his last two years.

IP-IL Philosophy is a systematic exposition of the Higher Wisdom with regard to the human soul. It is not based on any particular philosophy or religion. It stands on its own but it embraces all. I think after reading this exposition, remarks may be like the following made, "Yes, yes this is what we also say." But the charm of this exposition is that it puts the fundamental truth of life in a universally acceptable way - in simple words, in an orderly manner, focusing on the essentials and thereby preventing the reader from distractions. It also has new ideas in it.

The main body of this book has three divisions; namely, the View of Life, the Way of Life, and the Goal of Life. They explain what we need to understand, do, and expect respectively. The teachings are preceded with a message from God to all human beings.

This philosophy declares that we are in truth the offspring or sons of God: we resemble God and belong to Him wholly and solely although we think and experience ourselves as persons. What all religions call soul, this philosophy calls *Isvara Putra*, meaning the offspring or son of God. The words *Isvara Putra* do not refer to what we think we are but to what we really are the offspring or sons of God. Similarly, the words *Isvara Lila* do not refer to the usual meaning that goes with it, the great supernatural acts of gods and goddess but to what our lives really are, the play of God. According to this philosophy our everyday life is God's play. Wearing our body as His covering or mask, and assuming our ego as His dramatic role, God is playing our life as His sport or *Lila*. And through His play He is educating and evolving us, to experience our true identity that is not different from God, and at the same time evolving the world as well. This is the view of life declared by this philosophy and it has been explained in five fundamental truths.

This philosophy makes a clear distinction between individuals and persons. Individuals are *conscious beings* and persons are not. We are individuals. Persons are egos and egos are "I am so and so" thought. It is the first thought and is played by God. We identify ourselves with the body and think we are persons. This is a very subtle truth, which will get clearer and clearer in due course.

The reason we do not experience ourselves as the offspring of God but only as our physical body is due to a deluded attachment to our body, our ego, and our life. According to this philosophy the deluded attachment is not of our choice. It has been playfully created by God to remove our ignorance. Therefore, in one way the deluded attachment is a blessing in disguise. The deluded identification will continue until we realize the truth about our true identity. This is the way that God plays His divine drama and this is the meaning of our lives on earth. In a way it is like a father who is concerned about his son who has taken an overdose of sleeping pills. The father first inflicts suffering in various ways for example, by pouring cold water onto him to wake him. Then to sustain his wakefulness, the father introduces him to attractive objects, and when he is sure that his son had awakened sufficiently, he advises him to live unselfishly and finally makes him experience himself as the gentle son of the gentle father. Please don't stretch the analogy. The point is that the sleeper is made a dreamer to get awakened to his ever-attained wakefulness.

This philosophy prescribes Conscious Cooperation with God as the way of life to achieve the goal of life. Conscious Cooperation in brief is to be conscious of the five truths, as they have been explained in the view of life and to live one's life according to that truth. The wisdom for Conscious Cooperation is stated in the form of four spiritual practices. The first two are 'Right Awareness of the Five Truths' or *Satya Panchaka Samyak Gnana Abhyasa*, subjective and objective, and the last two are 'Righteous Living with a Service Spirit to God' or *Isvara Dasya Dharma Anushtana*, subjective and objective. The goal of life explains the fruits of the four spiritual practices. It is the 'Direct Experience of the Five Truths' or *Satya Panchaka Satya Gnanam*, subjective and objective.

Remaji has written hundreds of supplementary pages to this exposition. He has also explained each concept in various ways with stories and illustrations that can themselves be made into separate books.

The uniqueness of his teaching is that there is no separation between the theory, the practice, and the fruits of the practice. What you understand is what you practice and what you practice is what you experience. After experiencing the truth, there will be no need for further practice because the truth will become natural to you.

Because the message of this philosophy immediately uproots the ego without any compassion, some may find it difficult to grasp the teachings in the first reading itself.

However, repeated reading with an open mind will facilitate understanding.

Remaji's ideas are all interwoven and therefore it is not possible to explain all the intricacies of his writings in this handbook. Every important concept has several words to indicate it. Anyway, I suggest to the readers that if any ideas are not clear to you, just keep going: things will be explained. Also I request that you to be conscious of the following. Remaji has used several English words with meanings that he wants to convey that are not in the dictionary like knower, reknow, practisable, deludedly, impersonational ego etc. He also spells the Sanskrit word *jnana* as *gnana* for certain reasons of his own. So, please be open to letting the language speak for itself in a new way.

Repetition of words in a book can be a defect and in Sanskrit it is called *punarukti dosha*. But that defect is not applicable to this subject because our ignorance is ingrained in us so deeply that the ideas need repetition.

The depth of meaning of the ideas and words of this exposition is unfathomable. Each time we read or listen to the same words, they will give us a new meaning and they will open up our awareness to a deeper level. Great changes will take place in our understanding of things.

Personally, I have the satisfaction and joy of living in such a way that if all lived as I do a better world would come to be. If you asked me "What is that way?" "Living as a *conscious Isvara Putra* and the life a conscious *Isvara Putra* should live which will ultimately make me a perfect *Isvara Putra* or in other words, make me experience my ever-attained God-like Perfection" is my answer.

I surrender my humble efforts of introducing my Guru Remaji and his teaching to the world to my Guru himself, and beseech his grace to take care of it.

Remaji has said, "As I am to you, I am to everybody." I leave Remaji to speak to you through this exposition.

IP Meera Grimes
February 6th 2002

Preface

Dear Readers

Religion or Higher Wisdom with regard to the human soul asks us to aspire for our eternal welfare, which once attained will never be lost, and not to be wholly absorbed in the pursuit of transient worldly gains and satisfactions. Though the message of Higher Wisdom is primarily the way to attain eternal salvation, it is also of the highest importance in making our lives in the world better.

From the point of view of the individual, it is good because it gives him wisdom, firstly for suffering less and ultimately for suffering not at all. From the point of view of society, it is good because it induces individuals to behave better. It inspires and induces individuals to regulate their activities voluntarily in the general interest. Mere reliance on legislation for regulating individual behavior will be ineffective as it will only lead to a battle of wits between the lawmakers and the law breakers, and a proliferation of administrative machinery with all its attendant evil. It is not possible to control misbehavior by legislation and enforcement. Persuasion must support legislation and Higher Wisdom is the best persuader of socially desirable conduct. The more that Higher Wisdom is effective in *dharmarising* man's conduct, that is, in making individuals embrace righteous living, the less is the need for coercive legislation.

Unfortunately religion is not fulfilling its purpose of inducing good behavior. The mistake is not in the noble subject but in the improper understanding, teaching and practice of it. In a scientific and pragmatic modern mental climate, the message of the scriptures is not convincing. This is not the fault of the scriptures, but is due to the big time gap between the times in which the scriptures were promulgated and present times.

The question may be asked "What is the right understanding of the theory and practice of religion, which if taught will help man to suffer less and behave better?" My life is dedicated to this question. Through my writings I bring the essence of the message of the scriptures to the attention of modern man in a systematic, understandable, convincing, practisable way, in a manner hostile to none, criticizing none, and acceptable to all who love good reasoning and respect its findings.

I call my philosophy *Masquism.* At present I have no Indian name for it. I will refer to it as IP-IL philosophy, which stands for *Isvara Putra Isvara Lila Siddhanta,* where man or the individual is *Isvara Putra* meaning an offspring or son of God, and the life he or she lives is *Isvara Lila* meaning the play of God. It is a presentation of Higher Wisdom with regard to the human soul. It is not based on any book or person.

The great Buddha when he taught his *dharma* 2500 years ago said, "What I am teaching is nothing new. It is a restatement of an ancient ever-true wisdom." There have been and there are so many formulations of Higher Wisdom in this world.

The ever-true principle, *sanathana dharma* - true in the past, true today, and true in the future also, speaks regarding how a person born as a human being should live his life in this world. Fashions change and civilizations change but the ever-true principle does not change.

We live our lives somehow from birth to death. We live for pleasure or money or for fame and name. The ever-true principle states how life should be lived. My philosophy teaches the *way of life* based on the ever-true principle, which by so living one gets the highest reward of life: knowledge of one's true identity.

One can view this teaching in another way also. This exposition reconciles the teachings of Sankara and Ramanuja. It is like a bridge between advaita and visishtadvaita. It says, *Isvara,* the Lord is the reflection of

Brahman, the Unchanging Substratum, in the pure creative inexplicable power called *Maya*. The first transformation of *Maya* is called *mahat* meaning cosmic intellect. The cosmic intellect being pure and transparent, *Isvara*, the reflection of *Brahman* in the cosmic intellect *knows* His *Brahma Swarupa* or True Self and is the Lord of *Maya*. We, the individual conscious beings are also reflections of *Brahman* but in impure *Maya* or *antah-karana* meaning the inner instrument or the intellect of the individual. Because our intellects are impure or translucent but not transparent, we are not cognizant of our true Self and are subject to *Maya*. Thus our goal is Unchanging Substratum or *Nirguna Brahman*, and our Guide is *Isvara*, the *Saguna Brahman*.

I call the reflection of *Brahman* in cosmic intellect as *Isvara* and the reflections of *Brahman* in individual intellects as *Isvara Putra*s. In other words God is *Isvara* and souls are *Isvara Putra*s. To attain the realization, that we are *Isvara Putra*s belonging to God and resembling God is the penultimate great goal of life. To attain the realization, of our Substratum Self is the ultimate great goal of life.

Usually the scriptures of the world tell us that what will make us happy is not so much succeeding in the world but becoming freed from attachment to the world. But life has to be lived. So, I teach how to live in the world by which you will free yourself from attachment to the world. The foundation of this exposition is "We all are heavenly beings subject to delusion that we are earthly persons." From this truth the entire teaching arises. It teaches how heavenly beings can free them selves from the delusion that they are earthly persons and re-experience their heavenly estate.

I offer this exposition to mankind, which is a form of the eternal truth, for dynamising the whole world in a new living that will warm the heart of the great souls of the universe. I think it will meet the needs of the present generation, conditioned by the scientific and pragmatic values of the west.

The, presentation of this exposition functions in a way as a spokesman for all, and it serves as a key to the understanding of that perennial wisdom which is basic to the various religions of this country, India and also other countries. It is short and precise. Therefore I think it is easy to grasp and remember.

My exposition of the Higher Wisdom or Vedanta is not to compete with or supplant other expositions. My plans for a new spiritual social order are not to compete with or supplant other spiritual social movements. I only wish to give what I believe are greatly necessary: simple and broad guidelines. Without losing the simplicity, clarity, and catholicity of my wisdom, you are free to study any religion and participate in any movement.

Higher Wisdom

I define Higher Wisdom or *para vidhya* as the knowledge revealed by God in all religions. By Higher Wisdom I mean the soul of all religion which is not conditioned by the forms in which it is expressed. I am of the opinion that Higher Wisdom or Knowledge with regards to the human soul is *one*, although it wears different dresses in different lands, and with each dress it is called by a different name like Hinduism, Christianity and so on. I am not belittling the importance of the difference. I am only saying that there is a central common core among the wisdom of different religions.

Higher Wisdom is concerned about the wellbeing of human beings, and it tells us how to be free from suffering. But it may be said, "We have so many worldly remedies for suffering. We have food for the suffering of hunger, water for the suffering of thirst, the other sex for the suffering of sexual desire, medicine for sickness, fans for the heat of summer, and heaters for the cold of winter. What is unique about Higher Wisdom for ending suffering? The answer is this. Higher Wisdom offers you a radical and permanent freedom from suffering, and it assures you an eternal wellbeing. In this connection a biblical episode is relevant. Jesus was standing near a well where a woman was drawing water. Seeing Jesus she asked, "Do you want water to drink?" Jesus answered "The water which you can give, if I drink, I will thirst again. But I can give you a living water, which if you drink, you will never thirst again." It is remarkable that Jesus and the seers of the Upanishads speak in the same way.

Now what is the medicine that Higher Wisdom prescribes for the radical and permanent ending of suffering? The answer is simple. *Know the truth about what you know*. That is all. All that we have to do, to end all suffering radically and permanently is to simply know the truth about whatever we know.

To know things as they really are is called true knowing or knowledge or *yathartha gnana*. Sankaracharya says, "*Yathartha gnanam* or true knowledge ends all sorrow forever." Jesus also says, "Ye shall know the truth and the truth shall set ye free."

One may ask, "About what things sir, should one achieve true knowledge?" The answer is this. About whatsoever thing you achieve true knowledge, that thing will cease to afflict you with suffering. Don't you suffer in the knowing of yourself? Know the truth about yourself. Your suffering will cease. Do you suffer in the knowing of the adverse circumstances in your life? Know the truth about them. You will cease to suffer. Do you suffer in the knowledge of persons inimically disposed towards you? Know the truth about them. You will cease to suffer. Do you suffer in the knowledge of the desirable things of the world, which you want to get and cannot get? Know the truth about them, and you will cease to suffer. So according to Higher Wisdom, the object of living is right knowledge or true knowing, and not getting. Most people live for getting, and knowledge is to them a means for getting. If one wants to end all sorrow once and for all, one must reverse this. One must live, but *live to know rightly*.

Now we must be careful to understand what true knowledge means. According to Higher Wisdom, the word knowledge does not mean the knowledge which scientists are accumulating regarding various aspects of life. So let us proceed to understand the true import of the words true knowledge. A few examples may help.

A millionaire has received a bundle of notes total   ing several millions. His employees are busy counting them and piling them in proper heaps. Suddenly one employee cries "Sir, these notes are counterfeit. They are not real."

The boss examines them and agrees. They stop counting and piling up the money. They get up. Their interest in the notes has ceased because they have understood the *truth about the notes.*

A college student sleeping at night hears the noise of an object falling near his bed, and he puts on the light. He sees a wriggling snake. He is fearful of what kind of snake it is, whether it is poisonous or not, and he wonders how to deal with it. The snake watches him steadfastly. The boy's hair stands on end and he is perspiring. Then he sees the material of the snake's body. It is rubber. He prods the snake with a stick. The snake is lifeless. He picks up the snake and examines it. Inside there is a small note "Hope that snake amused you. With love, Gopal." The student has a hearty laugh and goes back to bed cogitating a trick to confound Gopal. Knowing that the snake is only a rubber snake is the true knowledge that liberated the student from fear.

It is a pleasant sunny morning, and you are taking your breakfast in the outer verandah looking at the street. A beggar comes and begs for food. You are annoyed and ask your servant to dispose of him with a *chapatti*, a dish like pita bread or two. But the fellow will not go. He wants a woolen coat for the winter. You can't stand his insolence. You leave your breakfast half eaten and step into the street and shout at the beggar. He shouts back louder. You are incensed. You fly into a rage, rush inside, grab a hockey stick and go out to teach the fellow a lesson. When you approach him, he looks at you with a seraphic smile, and you recognize, it is a friend playing an April fool's joke on you. You have achieved *true knowledge of the beggar.* Your problem has disappeared. Only amusement and pleasure is left.

Now let me tell you what the true knowledge is that Higher Wisdom speaks about. According to Higher Wisdom*, every person including yourself is a dramatic role played by God.* Therefore according to Higher

Wisdom, *to know every human being as a role Played by God is true knowledge*. This is not a poetic imagery but *a sober truth*.

In the stage of life, God is playing innumerable roles and each one of us (as persons) is a role that He is playing. Our suffering will end and will only end when we behold the Player in the play, especially in ourselves. This is the true knowledge that Higher Wisdom speaks about and it is not the empirical and scientific knowledge evolved by scientists. It is not that empirical and scientific knowledge has no relevance for the achievement of true knowledge. On the contrary, they have. Even in my own case science served its purpose by making me ask the question "How can the child be me?" Everyone who looks at the photographs of themselves as children, do not ask this question. I asked. Many had seen the apple fall but did not ask the question that Newton did. But Newton's question being objective did not transform his life, but only his understanding of objective nature. My question being subjective and fundamental changed my whole life. Thus, a scientific attitude has pervaded my entire life.

Now we have to go one step further. There are two aspects to true knowledge. One of the aspects we have noticed is to *see the Player in the play* and the other is to *see the stuff out of which the Player has fashioned whatever we see or the various roles He is playing*. The roles that God plays, i.e. the human body or the persona consist of hands and legs, eyes and ears and brain and mind and thoughts and feelings. All of these are fashioned by God out of *one-stuff*, which I call 'MA'. MA is the inexplicable Creative Power of God. The Vedanta calls it Maya. Maya means that illusion which has got the capacity to delude the beholder. Out of *one stuff* i.e. MA, God has fashioned the objects of the world like the sun, the moon, and the stars, mountains and rivers, and our person that consists of hands and legs, eyes and ears, and thoughts and speech etc.

The world that we live in and the body that we live with are fashioned by God and played by God. If we understand this truth and play the game of life with God, which means to live righteously or live in *dharma*, indifferent to the lesser prizes the world has to offer, and unafraid of the temporary hardships that may cross our path, the *Player will reveal Himself* to us. The game will end as far as we are concerned though it will continue for others.

We all know that after graduation from university we need not return to college to study again. Seeing the Lord and MA in the world, behind the forms is to graduate in the University of Life. If we accomplish this graduation, we need not be reborn here of necessity. A few graduates may *choose* in accordance with God's Will, to be reborn to help other students to achieve graduation quickly.

The play of life is really God playing at binding Himself and freeing Himself. It is like a child bored with his loneliness and lack of playmates, closing one fist, pretending that he cannot open his hand again and using the fingers of his other hand to open the fingers of this hand. God plays at blindfolding Himself and at removing the blindfold. He plays at hiding Himself and finding Himself. I have actually seen children doing this as some of you also have. So the play of life is really God becoming others so that He can enjoy loving and being loved. Wearing our bodies as His mask, and assuming our egos as His dramatic roles, God is playing our lives as His Sport. To put it in other words, God is the Impersonator and what we think we are is His impersonational ego and our bodies are His impersonation.

Now we are in a position to understand more precisely the statement "Every one of us is a role that God is playing."

The truth that we are all God pretending to be deluded by His own play, cannot be digested by all. So the Higher

Wisdom teaches another view of our condition which would be easier to comprehend than the one above. According to the truer statement of the Higher Wisdom every one of us is an eternal, immortal offspring or sons of God, but subject to an oblivion or total nescience. God, being deprived of the joy of the companionship with His children, has involved us in creation, and He has subjected us to a deluded identification with the roles, which He is playing. Through the challenges of life, He is impelling and compelling us to respond to them, and He is trying to awaken us from our primordial slumber.

Thus two views have been propounded. One is that we are God pretending to be deluded by His own play, which delusion is however, from our point of view, real, though from God's point of view it is feigned. The other view is that we are all the offspring or sons of God subject to a primordial nescience whom God is trying to awaken by involving us into births and deaths and impelling and compelling us to respond to the vicissitudes and challenges of life. The first view of life has been explained in "The Aphorisms of *Masquism*, and the second view of life in the IP-IL Philosophy. All the statements of this exposition are the truths of Higher Wisdom with regard to the human soul.

We are all offspring or sons of God, deluded by our divine Father's play, and it behoves us to live to *awake* and not to live to get more and better conditions and comforts in the state of delusion where we deem the play to be real. Now we have come of age. We should understand God's purpose for us, which is to awaken us from our primordial ignorance of our true identity, and to live cooperatively with Him to facilitate and expedite the fulfillment of His benign intention for us. *This is the meaning of life.*

Thus religion is God's invitation to human beings to consciously cooperate with Him in realizing the *great end* that He has for us.

My Life, Work, and Mission

My Life and Work

There are writings promoting clarity and order in human thinking. The lives of those whose minds function with clarity and order tend to promote wellbeing and order in the environment. I am living so that my writings, my talks, and my ideas may promote *order* in the most comprehensive sense of the term.

God always Act in order. Any disorder in nature is a part of the order. Man has to order his activities and his culture to accord with the natural order. Righteousness or *dharma* is the term for that comprehensive meaning of order. Ethical rectitude is only a small though an essential part of righteousness.

I hope to promote order by promoting order in human thinking. I hope to promote righteousness, in the world by persuading human beings to become lovers of righteousness, and to live a Pro-God righteous or *dharmic* life. In another way of speaking, my life is dedicated to teaching that which is revealed to me as simply and clearly as possible with numerous illustrations so that even young school children can understand it.

My Mission

It must be admitted that the religious scene has always been confused and contentious. My mission is to teach the basic fundamental principles of religion in as clear and universally acceptable a manner as possible to reduce confusion and contention. It is a restatement of the perennial truths of religion in a form, which I think, will serve the religious needs of the present skeptical and scientifically minded generation.

My mission is to *doctoral unity* to Hindus to start with and to all ultimately. In other words my mission is to unite all humanity in a *common view of life, way of life, and goal of life*. The message is not at all intended to displace existing religious teachings, existing concepts of God, or other methods of attaining God. Rather it is to classify, codify, and unify spiritual wisdom in the ultimate sense.

The world is a place for human beings to work and to earn the knowledge of their true identity, conducted by God, for the benefit of every individual, subjected to a beginning-less ignorance of one's true identity. The life you live is a pilgrimage of spiritual practice performed by you, though unknowingly. Your persona is the instrument of spiritual practice used by you, unknowingly. You are a pilgrim, walking towards the realization of your true identity in this world, which is a workshop for your spiritual endeavor, but unknowingly. God is your Guide, and Eternal Guru. Your goal is to attain the state of non-dual At-one-ment with God, and experience your Substratum Self or Perfection.

The world is a great university and God is the principal. We are the students, and education is being imparted to us through experiences we undergo through the instruments of cognition, volition and action. The realization of our true identity is the degree to be obtained so that we need not reenter the college again. In the above, both the view of life and the goal of life are stated,

The way of life is conscious and intelligent and earnest cooperation with God. I call this *conscious cooperative life with God*. The Sanskrit word for it is *Isvara Saha Yoga*. The *Conscious Cooperation* consists in *Right Awareness of the Five Truths*, and *Righteous Living with a Service Spirit to God* that has been expounded in these writings.

A word regarding
New Terminology

I am presenting a way of making this exposition easily understood so that, it can be assimilated by the West. By making use of certain western terminology, it will be helpful to everybody. Also I am fond of inventing words to evoke in the mind the understanding that I want. The new terminology that I am using will facilitate the understanding and practice of my philosophy. As I am hoping that this philosophy may get a world acceptance, and the West is going to receive many eastern words, I think it is proper for the East to receive some words from the West. You should know that the words have been selected to express the central truth in an easily understandable and rememberable form. The western terminology, at first reading, may appear somewhat strange but my experience is that after getting used to it, it will prove to be very useful in remembering a complex network of ideas.

I am using the words masque, masquerader, and mask, and I am adding some signification of my own. The words masque and masquerader are found in the English dictionary. The word masque means a play where the characters wear masks over their faces and their bodies. The word mask means covering. The word masquerader means the actor taking part in such a play. The players in the masque are called masqueraders.

Let me explain how I am using these words. For example, an actor Mr. X, acting as Hamlet, projects a new ego in a new body or costume, but behind this new ego and new body is his original ego and original body. The new ego presented I call the *rader* (pronounced as rayder), and the new body presented, I call the mask.

The original player I call *R<u>a</u>der* (pronounced as Raahder). The *Rader* is the real player behind the mask.

Now let me come to our real life. I call our physical body the mask. The word mask refers to both the physical body and the intellect. I call our physical body the outer mask and our intellect the inner mask. I call the person or ego the *rader* (pronounced as rayder). The *rader* is the apparent user of the mask so I call the person a *maskrader* meaning the apparent user of the mask or body. I am spelling the word as *maskrader* instead of masquerader, and designating his activities as a *maskrade* or *maskrading* instead of masquerade for certain good reasons, which will become clearer as we proceed. God, who is the real Player behind the mask, I call *R<u>a</u>der* (pronounced as Raahder) meaning the Player and the Manipulator. God is the Real Player in each mask as well as the Player of all the masks. I call the Player in each mask the *MaskR<u>a</u>der*, and the Player of the entire world the *MasqueR<u>a</u>de*r. I call the world Masque (pronounced as mask-q); the word masque represents the entire universe. There is only one *Rader*, but there are many *maskraders*. There is only One God but there are many roles.

According to this philosophy, *maskrading* is a very honorable and artistic activity of God through which God is simultaneously evolving the world and enlightening us. In another way of putting the same idea is this. God is the Impersonator; the world and our physical bodies are God's impersonations, and the apparent person is God's impersonational ego. So please remove from your mind the association of the word masquerading with its usual meaning which means pretending or acting falsely. I have no better word than this to employ.

Now the question can be asked, "If God is the Player or *R<u>a</u>der* and the egos are the played roles or *maskraders*, then what are we?" The answer is that we are offspring or sons of God. More precisely we are the reflections of God in the intellect. I call what all religion means by soul '*Isvara Putra*'. I don't have a new western terminology for the soul. You are really a soul, an offspring or son of God or an *Isvara Putra*. You are between God or *MaskRader*, and ego or *maskrader*, ignorant of God, whom you resemble, and deludedly identified with the ego, which is a played role of God.

Your physical body is the mask of God. Your person is the played role or *maskrader* of God. Your life is the play or *maskrade* of God. You are really an offspring or son of God or an *Isvara Putra*, but think you are a person. Your goal does not lie in succeeding as a person or *maskrader*, but in awakening to your real identity, which is not different from God or *MaskRader*.

TERMINOLOGY

POPULAR	NEW	VEDANTIC
God	*R<u>a</u>der*	*Isvara*
Soul	*Isvara Putra*	*Isvara Putra*
Ego or Person	*Rader*	*Isvara N<u>a</u>taka Patram*
Physical Body	*Mask*	*Isvara Vesham*
World or Universe	*Masque*	*Isvara Lila*
Activities of the World	*Masquerade*	*Isvara Lila*
Activities of Persons	*Maskrade*	*Isvara Lila*
Substratum Self	RA	*Brahman*
God's Creative Power	MA	*M<u>a</u>y<u>a</u>*
God in each Body	*MaskR<u>a</u>der*	*Antary<u>a</u>mi*
God in all Bodies	*MasqueR<u>a</u>der*	*Sarv<u>a</u>ntary<u>a</u>mi*

PRONUNCIATION

Masque – pronounced as mask-q

Rader – pronounced as rayder

Maskrader – pronounced as maskrayder

R<u>a</u>der – pronounced as Raahder

MaskR<u>a</u>der – pronounced as MaskRaahder

MasqueR<u>a</u>der – pronounced as mask-q-Raahder

Isvara – pronounced as Eshvara

A word on
Self Regarding Conception

The ego is the sense of an affirmation of a self-hood in the psychophysical construction. I am a man, I am a woman, I am educated, I am a Brahmin, I am an Indian, I am an American, I am a law abiding citizen - all these are expressions of the ego. Except for the liberated ones, all are egoists. The good and the bad, the sinner and the virtuous, are all egoists.

In the ultimate analysis, egoism is a state of delusion but egoism plays a vital part in human evolution. Egoism can be defined as the experience of pleasure in ego-contemplation. To derive satisfaction from the idea "I am so and so" is egoism. Egoism is an important instrument for God or Nature in evolving us. Egoism is the drive to approve oneself. The level of approval will go on increasing until there is an irrepressible desire for perfection and one becomes a true seeker of perfection.

Like everything else, however, egoism can take unwholesome forms. For example, the desire or craving for being praised is such an unwholesome form. When egoism is developed, a strong craving for a Self Regarding Conception, which will enhance one's ego satisfaction arises. There is a craving for a concept, which will enhance our Self Regarding Conception and thus our egotistic wellbeing. It is this craving that drives people to join various organizations like Rotary Clubs, etc and makes one succumb to flattery. Political demagogues know how to exploit this craving amongst their followers.

Our wellbeing is related not only to our material and social living conditions but also to the way that we regard ourselves. Not only our wellbeing but also the quality of our living and the manner of our performance of our tasks is related to our Self Regarding Conception. When I became clearly aware of the truth of the constitution of the world and man's place in it, I felt that human beings should be given a True and New Self Regarding Conception from which a new life would flow naturally.

ISVARA PUTRA meaning an offspring or son of God is the truest and greatest of all Self Regarding Conception of human beings because we are really *Isvara Putra*s, the reflections of God in the intellect. The *Isvara Putra* concept exalts the human being's self respect. It is universally acceptable to people belonging to all religions and to all countries. It accords with the world's best wisdom which makes life sweeter and which can inspire happier and cooperative living. So be proud that you are an *Isvara Putra,* and don't go for lesser and false Self-Regarding Conceptions. *Isvara Putra* is not a label: it is what all of us really are. It is a revelation of a human being's inner and deeper constitution.

But it is one thing to know that one is an *Isvara Putra,* and another to experience oneself as one. To experience oneself as an *Isvara Putra,* one will have to love God as a good son or daughter, and serve Him as a good servant of His world. The *Isvara Putra* concept will impel a person to follow a noble life. There are enemies for the *Isvara Putra* to vanquish but the enemies are not outside of us. The enemy lurks within us. Desire, anger, stinginess, pride, and jealousy are the five enemies to be vanquished before the prize of the experience of oneself as an *Isvara Putra* can be gained.

When you love someone very much you want him to have the best. Nothing less than the best is good enough for the one you truly love. When you consider that something less than the best is good enough for somebody, you do not truly love him. You only like him. I say, *love yourself truly*. Desire the best for yourself. Desire the knowledge of your true identity or *Isvara Putra gnanam* for yourself. If you crave recognition by society as an important person, you are not seeking the best for yourself, and you do not truly love yourself. I don't say do not work for a good position in society. I say don't crave it. If you truly love yourself then nothing less than the non-dual Union or At-one-ment with God should be good enough for you. The experience of fullness of God-relationship in a non-dual At-one-ment with God is your ultimate highest good. It is Perfect Spiritual Health.

Dear Reader

I love you more wisely than you love yourself and therefore I am calling you. You are an *Isvara Putra*. Resolve to experience yourself as one. If you are an advocate for non-dualistic philosophy or advaita vedantin, please understand that the knowledge of one's Substratum Self or *Brahman*, and the knowledge of one's true identity as not different from God or *Isvara Putra* gnana, are not opposed. While very advanced spiritual practitioners can make a straight bid for non-dualistic experience, others will do well to seek first the experience of oneself as not different from God, and afterwards go to non-dualistic experience.

I inform all of you that you are offspring or sons of God or *Isvara Putra*s, even if you do not know it. I am inviting you to become good sons of God, or *conscious Isvara Putras*. Here I would like to say this.

Every soul is an Isvara Putra. Souls are heavenly beings and they don't have sex like earthly mortal persons. The relation between God and soul is the most intimate, not less than husband and wife. I am choosing Father and son relationship for general acceptance. The right to call your true identity as Mrs. God, or Miss God, or Master God or in other words *Isvara Patni* or *Isvara Bharya* or *Isvara Putri* or *Isvara Putran*, is yours.

According to this philosophy both men and women in truth are *Isvara Putras.* How should *Isvara Putras* live so that they can become perfect offspring or sons of God or *Isvara Putras*? I am answering the question through this exposition.

God's Address to Mankind

I, the Creator of the world, am present in every one of you, as an Inner Ruler and Controller or *Antaryami.* You are My offspring or *putras*, object of My loving paternal concern. You are God's sons or *Isvara Putras* belonging to Me and resembling Me, Immortal and Perfect, altogether different from the mortal imperfect bodies you indwell and live with.

I know you as My sons. You do not know Me as your Father. But even then you ARE My sons. I want that you should know in your own direct experience that you are God's sons or *Isvara Putras.* To know that you are *Isvara Putras*, in your own direct experience is your highest good. There is no higher attainment possible. After knowing you are *Isvara Putras,* you will not be reborn.

Isvara Putras are of three kinds, ordinary, good and Perfect. Ordinary sons or *Isvara Sadharna Putras* are those who do not know they are *Isvara Putras* or knowing are not interested in realizing their real identity. Good sons or *Isvara Suputras* are those who want to realize their true identity. Perfect sons or *Isvara Sat Putras* are those who have realized their true identity.

My body or *sarira* will ever tease you, till you know Me and become one with Me, within you. Give up trying to woo My body. They will betray you willingly or unwillingly because, I am its Inner Controller. You can know Me, and progress in At-one-ment with Me by remembering Me as your Inner Ruler and Controller or *Antaryami*, and Eternal Father or *Parama Pita*, and yourself as My offspring or *Isvara Putra*, and do all that you do as Service to Me, the Cosmic Person or *Jagath-Sariri*. When you achieve At-one-ment with Me, you will have achieved At-one-ment with everyone else, and everything else.

The above is a short summary of ALL RELIGIOUS WISDOM. I know because I uttered them.

VIEW OF LIFE

Right Understanding of the Five Truths Consists of Sections P, Q, R, S, T, U and V

INTRODUCTION

The Player, the Play and the Played for - in these terms the world-view is comprehended. These are the three great substances or *tattva thraya.* They stand for God, the world, and the soul and this is the meaning that God is playing His divine sport for the sake of His offspring, the souls.

I define God, subjectively, as the Unchanging Awareness in an individual, and objectively, as the Creator, Player, and Director of the world process. I have given God no form or name but I have given God a designation, the true and the best designation - that of the Player of the divine sport and the Director of the world organization.

I define the divine play of God as the act that has been performed effortlessly, gracefully, and beautifully without any selfish motive.

The one who suffers the play and is ignorant of the Player is the soul. God is the Player, the world is His divine play and the souls are the played for.

God is the Creator, the world is His creation and the souls are the offspring or sons of the Creator.

God is the Director, the world is His organization and the souls are the unconscious servers of God.

There is God, there are souls, and there is the world. One God plays innumerable roles non-stop, to awaken the souls. For the souls to understand this and live cooperatively with God is to live religiously.

In Sanskrit the three great substances are called Isvara, *Isvara Lila*, and *Isvara Putra*. *Isvara* means the Lord. Lila means divine sport. *Isvara Lila* means God's divine sport or play. *Putra* means offspring or son and *Putras* mean offspring or sons. *Isvara Putra*s therefore means the offspring or sons of God. That is the Lord is playing His sport for the sake of His offspring or son is the meaning of life.

According to my new terminology *Rader*, the Great Player is *maskrading* for the sake of the souls or *Isvara Putra*s.

I don't have a new name for the soul. The soul is *Isvara Putra*.

SECTION P

Five Truths Pertaining to You: Subjective

Understand the Truth Pertaining to God
Understand the Truth Pertaining to Your Self
Understand the Truth Pertaining to Your Body
Understand the Truth Pertaining to Your Person
Understand the Truth Pertaining to Your Life

Understand the Truth Pertaining to God

In this section the truth about God and the various aspects of God are explained. This will help you to better understand God's relationship to you and to the world. It will also help you to go deeper into the meaning of God, which will enable you to commune with Him and contemplate Him directly without any outside help.

My philosophy uses the terms *Rader*, which means the Player, or *Isvara*, which means the Lord, for God. God is *Rader* and *Rader* is *Isvara*. Until you get used to the new terminology, you can use the one that is already familiar to you and add that meaning to the new terminology.

RA Has Become the Player

In the beginning there was RA, and with Him was MA. RA is the Unchanging Awareness and MA is the Creative Power. I call the Absolute/Substratum Self/Pure/Infinite Consciousness RA. When creation is imminent RA, the Unchanging Awareness reflects in MA, the Creative Power. I call the reflection of RA in MA as *Rader*, meaning the Player. When RA reflects in MA as *Rader*,

MA experiences a quickening and begins to transform and creation starts.

According to Vedanta RA is *Brahman*, MA is *Maya* and Rader is *Isvara*.

God/*Rader*/*Isvara* is the First coming down of RA

If *avatar* means a "coming down," then Rader, the Player Himself is the first *Avatar* of RA. RA, the Unchanging Awareness as it were has jumped, descended into the ocean of MA, the Creative Power, as *Rader*, the Player, where we, the souls, are floundering to rescue us from our primordial slumber.

RA, the Unchanging Awareness reflected in MA, the Creative Power as Rader, of course chooses to marry MA and as it were, has become her husband, and father the creation. If It/He did not so reflect, we, the souls cannot be rescued. So Rader, the Player can be considered the first coming down or *avatar* of RA, active to rescue us who are drowned in primordial slumber.

God/*Rader*/*Isvara* is Great Reflection of RA in MA

It has been said that *Rader* is the first reflection of RA, in MA. As MA, the Creative Power in which RA, the Unchanging Awareness is reflected, is pure, the reflection knows the original. Therefore *Rader* or the Player is Master of MA, the Creative Power.

We, the souls are also equally the reflections of RA, in MA, but the portion of the MA in which we are reflected, is not a pure substance, though it is pure enough to reflect. Therefore, we, the reflections of RA are subject to a loss of the experience of the original, and therefore we are under the influence of MA, the Creative Power.

Let me explain. Daylight falls equally on all objects in the daytime but it only enters into, penetrates, or is reflected by objects like water, glass, etc that are transparent. The daylight does not reflect on objects like trees, buildings etc that are not transparent. Similarly, RA, the Unchanging Awareness, which is Infinite Consciousness though omnipresent, reflects only in pure substance.

The Vedanta refers to God as *Maha Chidabhasan*, meaning the Great Reflection of the Infinite Consciousness. *Maha* means great, *Cit* means consciousness and *abhasa* means reflection.

Love Has Become the World

The nature of RA, the Unchanging Awareness is indescribable. But roughly we can say that RA is Infinite Consciousness and *Rader*, the Player is Self-Consciousness. RA is Love Itself and *Rader* Loves Himself. God, whom I call *Rader*, wanting to love others becomes the world, which I call *Masque*. The world is God's *Masque* and the *Masque* is *Isvara Lila* meaning God's play.

God/*Rader*/*Isvara* is Both Efficient and Material Cause of Creation

When RA, the Unchanging Awareness reflects in MA, the Creative Power as *Rader*, the Creative Power begins to transform and the cosmic intellect is the first transformation.

According to Vedanta the transformation takes place in the following way. From the cosmic intellect issued the five subtle substances namely space, air, fire, water and earth. They have three qualities. They are transparent, translucent, and opaque or *sattva*, *rajas*, and *tamas*. To put it roughly, the inner instrument or intellect and the five sense organs were formed out of the transparent part of the five subtle substances. The life breath and the five organs of action are formed from the translucent part of the five subtle substances. Then, after undergoing quintuplication of the opaque part of the five subtle substances, the physical body and its components of flesh, bone, blood, etc and the components of the physical world like the mountains, rivers, etc are fashioned. Therefore, R<u>a</u>der or God is both efficient and the material cause of all existence otherwise known as creation.

God/*R<u>a</u>der/Isvara* is the Creative Conceiver and the Invisible Player

God is the Creative Conceiver of all that you know. He has conceived the stage, which is the universe, the stage properties, which are the objects in the universe and also the actors, that is all the different living beings in it. What you think you are that is your body is created and played by God. The infinite intelligence, which is behind the construction and maintenance of the physical body you live with, and the Infinite Love and Intelligence which is behind your thinking-suffering consciousness and which is evolving you through Its/His play is God. The infinite and invisible Player chooses to sport as the finite and the visible, and has become the World. He is All Pervasive and at the same time He is within every individual and works in secret. But His works are manifest.

All that constitutes the play by way of the physical bodies, minds, thoughts, feelings, emotions, and memories are all modes of MA, the Creative Power of God. The Vedanta calls it by various names such as *Maya*, *Prakriti*, *Pradhan*, and *Avidhya*, meaning a mysterious something, which is neither real nor unreal.

Because God is the Maker of the universe, He is also the Owner or the Boss and the Director of the universe. He is the Owner of everything that exists including ourselves, and all that we possess. He is the Inner Ruler and Controller or *Antary<u>a</u>mi* of each individual and also Inner Ruler and Controller of the universe, or *Sarv<u>a</u>ntary<u>a</u>mi*. He is the instigator of the individual's psychophysical activities and the illuminator of our mental process. He is the controller, activiser and indweller of every thing and the animator of the physical and mental bodies. The laws that control the universe operate under the direction of God.

I said that our physical bodies are created, maintained, and played by God. We can understand this in a way by watching an infant. Who has made that wonderful body? The parents did not make the body. The body is the creative construction of God, the great Conceiver. Who is maintaining it? It is God. Take the activities of the infant. Who is doing it? Does the infant know what it is doing? Does the baby know it is smiling beautifully? No, but it smiles. When a girl sees a man that she loves, her eyes light up. Who is doing the lighting up of the eyes? Does the girl light up her eyes consciously? No, it is the play of God and the Player is invisible in the play.

From an old body, with shriveled skin, comes a sweet young baby with petal-like skin. Where does it come from? From where does youth eternally renew? Who continually conquers death? Does the rose flower come out of an ugly little seed or from God within the seed? The experience of thrills of happiness, where do they come from? Whose intelligence is at work in the fact that in the soft fruits the seeds are so hard that the birds will reject them? It is from the Great Manipulator, the invisible Player of course.

God/*R̲ader*/*Isvara* is the Greatest of Actors and the Universe is His Artistic Expression

The world is God's drama or *Isvara Lila*. Wearing our physical bodies as His mask just as human actors wear their costumes and masks, God is playing various roles as what every one thinks as he or she is. Every living being is a dramatic role that God is playing. In that way, we are all roles of God that God is sporting on the world stage.

God is the greatest of actors. I will give some special reasons for saying this. I will also tell you some of the differences between a human drama and God's drama. Human actors can play only one role at a time. True, they can play different roles, but not at the same time. But God is playing innumerable roles at the same time and non-stop for thousands of years. Man's drama lasts only for a few hours. Nowadays there are non-stop cinemas and the audience can enter and leave when they like. In human drama the audience and the drama are separate and they do not interfere with each other. Also a human drama has only a few characters. But God's drama is spread over the whole world. There are billions of characters and the drama is non-stop from the beginning of time to the end of time. All of these are differences in time and space but the main difference is that the actors are also audience and the audience that is the spectators are also actors in God's drama. There is double acting, a non-deluded, non-suffering single actor of all roles, and many deluded, suffering actors, all separate, and all distinct. The beauty is that the deluded actors do not know that they are deluded actors. The liberated one's are undeluded, non-playing Witness of God's drama.

God acts from fullness in Love and the world is God's creative art. Every activity that takes place in this world is God's artistic expression. If you are slouching in an easy chair, and tired, God is playing slouching in an easy chair feigning tiredness. If you feel fine, God is playing that mood. If you suffer a headache, God is playing at having it. If you are vicious God is playing as vicious. He dances as the peacock. He stings as the scorpion. He loves as Jesus. He destroys as Genghis Khan. He kills as the cat, and He lets himself be killed as the mouse.

The activities of the world and our life in it IS God's *Play*, and *God's* play. This is not a view; it is the *Truth*.

The Player is also the Witness of His Play

It has been said that God has become the world. This means that the world is God's form or *rupa*. But God's true Self or *Swarupa* is different from His form. God's true Self is RA, the Unchanging Illuminating Consciousness, and as RA, He is the Witness of His play. God is playing as the world and at the same time, He is also witnessing His play. Therefore God is both the Player and the Witness of His play or *Kridi* and *Sakshi*.

God has two aspects: the transcendental and immanent. The transcendental aspect is RA, the Unchanging Awareness and the immanent aspect is Rader, the Cosmic Player or Cosmic Consciousness. God as the Player, and God as the Absolute are closely related, but they must be distinguished. When the sun shines, the lotus opens. The sun does not open the lotus. The sun does not touch the lotus. Similarly God's true Self is quite apart from the play, though playing it. If you remove the play, you will see the Player, the Seed of the creation. God as an Absolute, is the Witness of His play. As an Absolute, God is not judgeable or definable as being so and so. But still the terms Truth, Consciousness, and Bliss are selected to indicate His Absolute Self.

God is both the Knower of His true Self, which is RA, and also knows the truth about the entire phenomenon as His play. The world is not God, but it is God's play. The activities are not God's doing but they are played by God. Though the world and our lives are the play of God, He is not in the play. To the contrary - the play is in God. How? As our thoughts are inside us, the world, which is God's mental activity, is inside Him.

Our true identity is also Witness. But we, instead of remaining a non-playing Witness of God's play are now deludedly claiming it as our lives, and thus we suffer pain and pleasure.

God/*R<u>a</u>der*/*Isvara* is a Cosmic Person

God is a Person or *Purusha*, but He is a Superior Person or *Purushottama*. As our physical body is our person, the entire world is God's Person, which includes our bodies also. God is the Cosmic Person: we are individual persons.

God is defined as being associated with the world and that includes all the creatures living in it and also inanimate objects just as we are associated with a particular body. God is superior in the magnitude of His body but He is different from us in the way that He is associated with His Cosmic Body. Firstly, He is not qualified by it, as we are. Secondly, and this is suggested in the first, His association with the Cosmic Body is free and therefore, He has absolute mastery over it. We are bound to our bodies.

All the objects of the known are God's forms or masks and all the activities including ours are God's play or *maskrades* or *Isvara Lila*. God is there as everything and everyone. Every object in the world - trees, plants, rivers, etc are God's form. The sun is His form. The sunshine and its heat are His play. Every stone is His form. The falling rain is His play. Wind is His form. Storms are His play. Hurricanes are His play. Earthquakes are His play. He plays as stones, rocks, worms, insects, snakes, alligators, birds, animals, savages, rouges, good people, high-class human beings etc. God has become the world. God is standing there as trees, floating there as clouds, falling down as rain, grunting as the rhinoceros, and screaming as playing children. Every human and sub-human body is God's form and He is behind every form, animating them. Each one of us is sensitive to our own body but God is sensitive to every body, because He experiences the world as His body. The Cosmic Person is right behind you, the individual person.

Try to see the formless God in all forms. When the formless attracts you more than the forms, you are spiritually growing.

God/*R<u>a</u>der*/*Isvara* Resides in Your Heart

Though God, the Player is literally everywhere, He resides in your heart, and is residing in everyone's hearts. He is deep within you. He is the inner sun, shining in everybody's Heart always, whether one knows it or not. He never sleeps.

God is your Heart, and you are in Him. So in one way of speaking, from your Heart, the entire play or *Lila* emanates. All things are, and all things take place in your Heart. The drama of bondage and liberation take place in the Heart. God, you, and the divine sport are all in the Heart. God is the Light of the heart and the Light of the world. By His Light, the outer sun shines. The *gayatri* mantra says, "The Light that lights up the sun shines in your intellect." God is the Light in your intellect. He is the dispeller of darkness in your heart and He makes it resplendently bright. Jesus said, "Let your Heart be full of Light."

God/*R<u>a</u>der*/*Isvara* is the Only Eternally Liberated One

God is the only eternally liberated One or *Nitya Mukthan*. Others are once bound and then they become liberated due to God's help. God is ever with you as your Eternal Father and Inner Ruler and Controller or *Antary<u>a</u>mi*. It is very good to contemplate God as the ever-liberated One.

God/*R<u>a</u>der*/*Isvara* is Your Eternal Guru

God is the source of all wisdom, and love. He is playing at being each one of us, and He is educating us, and awakening us through His play. He is our eternal enlightener or *Guru*. He is the First Guru of all of us. He controls us, teases us, excites us, frightens us, soothes us, scratches us, embraces us, and crushes us, through His play and by that, He is removing our ignorance of our true identity, and our deluded identification with our bodies. But many sleeping sons and daughters do not want to be disturbed. They say, "Help us to have pleasant dreams or go to hell." Those children are thickly deluded.

God is the Player of the world, and we are the played for. God is the teacher, and we are the students. God is the doctor, and we are the patients. God is the educator, and we are the learners.

God/*R*ader/*Isvara* is Your Inseparable companion

God is inseparably in union with you as the sustainer of your consciousness, as the instigator and impeller of your emotions and volition, and as the illuminator of your subjective cognition. Unless He sustains your consciousness, you cannot know. Unless He activates you, you cannot act. He is unknown by you, but He enables you to know all that you know, think all that you think, and feel, experience, speak, and do all that you, feel, experience, speak, and do.

God/*R*ader/*Isvara* is the Lawful Governor and Grace Bestower

All are God governed whether one likes it or not, and whether one knows it or not. God governs us according to the choices that we make in our living. He is the lawful governor but behind His governing there is Grace, because He works through His government to liberate us. Our delusion distorts the flow of His Grace. If we make ourselves God's by following the truths, His conduction will direct our activities. The mother holds and presses the crying child in the bath water, and she will not stop pressing, until, all the dirt is washed off. Similarly, God has involved us in the "I am a person" deluded life and until our ignorance and delusions are removed, He will be involving us in the earthly life. He has made us a thinker and is also controlling our thoughts.

God/*R_ader*/*Isvara* is Your Eternal Father

I said that RA, the Absolute is Love, and the Self-Love of God is connected with RA. Self-Love and love of others can combine as they do in the love of a father for his son. The father loves his son and in that love for his son he loves himself. God is our Eternal Father or *parama pit_a*. The earthly parents are His representatives. God, is not only our Eternal Father, but is also everything to us. He is the only real relative of all of us.

In the sense that both God and we are reflections of RA, in one manner of speaking, we are brothers, He being the enlightened Big Brother who helps us the little unenlightened brothers to get enlightened. In another manner of speaking, God is the Father, working for the disentrancement of his offspring. Yet in another manner of speaking, God is like Mother, at work to restore us, the children or offspring of RA who are estranged from the Father, back to the Father.

God/*R_ader*/*Isvara* is Your Real Home

God's home is Heaven or *param dh_ama*. The earth is God's workshop where the souls are being prepared to be fit to enter Heaven. If earth were a happy place, nobody would want to go to Heaven. Even now when the earth is full of misery, few want to go to Heaven. Experience of God and experience of Heaven are the same. It is really very sad that Heaven, the Eternal, True,

All Auspicious Realm is as nothing for ordinary sons of God, and the untrue, pain and pleasure mixed earth is everything for them.

I say, if you understand the Five Truths and work on the Four Spiritual Practices sincerely, what is now dark will one day become so bright that what, is bright now will become a shadow. In other words you will see the Player in the play.

Understand the Truth Pertaining to yourself

This section explains the truth about you, the individual. It says that you are really an offspring or son of God or an *Isvara Putra*, but deludedly think that you are a mortal person. It explains the concept of *Isvara Putra* in various ways and helps you to understand the truth about your true identity, your relationship to God, and to the world.

You are an Offspring or son of God

It has been said in the previous section that God is playing a dramatic role as what you think your are. Now you may ask "If I am not the Player and also not the played role, then who am I?" I say, you are an offspring or son of God or an *Isvara Putra*, who suffers the play of God due to the ignorance or *agnana* of your true identity, and the subsequent delusion or *moha* regarding the play. Let me explain.

An actor called Ram acts as Sam. Sam is a poor businessman. Sam is just a role that Ram is playing. Sam is only a mode, a thought or a *bhava* in Ram's mind. That is all. Sam is not an individual. He is a role in the mind of Ram. He has no existence apart from Ram's mind. When Ram acts as Sam, Ram does not suffer because Ram knows that he is really Ram and not the poor Sam. Ram is conscious that Sam is only a fictitious entity in his mind and there is no real individual such as Sam. Similarly in your life, God, the Player does not suffer. The played role, which is your person or ego, cannot suffer because it is just a mental mode in God's mind. But there is suffering and it is obvious that you are the sufferer. Who are you? I say, you are an offspring or son of God, deludedly thinking that you are a mortal person, which is the played role of God. Your suffering will end permanently only when you know that you are an offspring or son of God and not the mortal person.

Of this great universe, there is a Creator. You belong to Him as His offspring or son. I call the offspring or son of God *Isvara Putra*. *Isvara* means the Lord and *Putra* means the offspring or son. You are in truth an *Isvara Putra*, an immortal, perfect God-like Being, resembling God and belonging to God wholly and solely. As *Isvara Putra*, you have the fortune of serving God forever. You don't know this but by not knowing that you are immortal and perfect, you do not cease to be immortal and perfect and become mortal and imperfect. You may think and experience yourself as an imperfect mortal person but you are not one.

You resemble God as His son. By son I mean that you and God are the same kind or *sajatiya*, but you and your body are not same kind. The word son does not indicate to the physical body. The physical body is God's mask but you are an *Isvara Putra*. Philosophically speaking, both God and you are reflections of RA, the Unchanging Awareness, in MA, the Creative Power, but He in pure MA and you in impure MA. So God feels for you as a father reflection, or as a co-reflection. He loves you as a father loves his offspring and He is removing your ignorance through His divine play. Therefore you should learn to regard yourself as an offspring or son of God or

Isvara Putra and regard God as your divine Father and love Him and serve Him.

Emotionally speaking, you are the son or daughter of God. Let me explain. The child in his early years resembles his father in facial and behavioral characteristics but he is also unlike his father, because he is small and weak while his father is big and strong. But the child inherits the potentialities for growing up and becoming like his father, big and strong. The father too, impelled by parental love wants to develop his son to attain his own likeness and become big and strong. The son, impelled by his own innate nature as a good son, cooperates with his father by loving him and obeying his instruction.

Very similar is the relationship between God and you. God knows you as His offspring and He wants you to know Him as your Eternal Father and yourself as His offspring. He wants you to experience the fullness of your relationship with Him in a non-dual At-one-ment with Him. To this end, He has conjoined you with a mortal body. So, *Isvara Putra* is your true identity of which you are now ignorant. To love God, to delight in doing His Will by accepting His dispensations with equanimity, is your innate nature or *swadharma*. I want you to cherish the Father and son or daughter relationship more than the part and whole relationship. To understand that you are an *Isvara Putra*, resembling God but deludedly identifying with a body and an intellect which are really adjunct to you, and that is the *starting point of wise living*.

All of us are *Isvara Putra*s, belonging to God and resembling Him, although we do not have the experience as such. We may each think and experience ourselves as a mortal person qualified by a name, form, age, sex etc but we are all *Isvara Putra*s, including even the worst sinners. In short, all human beings are *Isvara Putra*s, whether they are Christians, Muslims, Jews, Sikhs, Hindus, Buddhists, communists, or atheists, etc.

You are placed Between the Player and His Play

Now the question arises, "If I am not the body, but an offspring or son of God, how have I come to be conjoined with my body in the condition of deluded identification with it? I don't remember having done it myself, but neither could the body, which by itself is inert, has done it."

The Vedanta answers, "God, the Creator who is ever present with you as your Inner Ruler and Controller or *Antaryami* has done it." God has conjoined you with your body to cure your disease of not knowing your true identity, which is a beginningless condition but an uncaused condition. You are placed between the Player and His play. You are deluded by the play, which is in front of you and ignorant of the Player who is behind your knowing consciousness.

Fact and Truth about You

The facts about you and the Truth about you are different. Name, form, age, sex, social status, income etc. are the facts about you. In short the mortal person is only a fact about you but not the Truth about you. In truth the mortal person is a dramatic role played by God to enable you to know what you really are. *Isvara Putra* is what the Truth of you and all human beings as well. You are a *conscious being* but your person is not.

Things are not always what they seem to be. For example, the water appears to be there, in the desert, but there is no water really there. It is a mirage. The water seen is only a deceiving appearance and not really real. In a similar way you too are not what you think you are. What you think you are and what you really are is altogether different. Identification with the body makes you think it is your identity, but it is not. The attributes of the psychophysical personality are not yours whether your personality is beautiful like Adonis or deformed. The Truth about you is perfect and unchanging while the facts about you are imperfect and change.

You have two choices: to live, believing in identity with the facts about yourself, trying to be as happy as possible until death, or to live to realize the Truth about your Immortal, Perfect, Changeless Being. When you live in the former way, you will alternatively be experiencing pleasure and pain, but fulfillment will elude you. When you live in the later way, you will live your life best because you have been ushered into a mortal existence to realize your true being.

You are also a Reflection of RA

Earlier I said that you are a conscious being and not the body. Now I say more precisely that you are a reflection of RA, the Unchanging Awareness, in the translucent intellect or buddhi which is a mode of MA, the Creative Power of God. In Vedanta the reflection of RA is called chidabhasan, meaning the reflection of the Infinite Consciousness. A reflection cannot but reflect the nature of the original. It reveals that your true identity is not different from God, but you don't have the experience of it now due to your beginningless ignorance. You are now a deluded reflection. There is only One great reflection of the Unchanging Awareness, in the pure mode of the Creative Power (cosmic intellect) who is God or Rader and a myriad of reflections of the Unchanging Awareness in the impure modes of the Creative Power (individual intellects), who are we, the souls.

The similarity and difference between God and you as reflections is this. God and you are both reflections of RA and Consciousness. However, God identifies with all bodies but you identify with only one. God knows His true Self, but you do not. God knows the world as not different from Him, but you don't. God identifies with the bodies without delusion but your identification with the body is with delusion. The point to be understood here is this. There are really no degrees of Consciousness. Consciousness is Unchanging Blissful Being. But there are degrees of your experience of Consciousness. Sugar's taste is always the same, but cakes will taste more or less sweet according to the amount of sugar present in them.

You are a Soul

You are an embodied soul, and not the body. The body is a construction of matter but you are not. Souls can never be other than immortal and perfect. I call the soul *Isvara Putra*.

In my younger days, I was impatient with the word soul. I thought it stood for a fictitious entity. Now I find it is a very useful concept: by cherishing which we can separate from matter and integrate with God. The soul can mate with God: the mind cannot. This is the truth to be clearly understood. You *are* a soul, though enveloped by a mind and a body, and enamored of them. You are enamored of the paramour, the played role of God. Your task is to experience the soul, and not so much in perfecting yourself as a mental physical personality though it has got its own place in the spiritual endeavor. Your main task is to divest yourself of the covering mind and to allow your soul-nature to express itself.

God-like Perfection is the soul's eternal nature, and to this nature the soul is now asleep. The soul actually has no nature being beyond nature. But as an offspring of God, it/you can manifest divine qualities through body and mind of pure substance. The soul is between God and the world. Both are pulling the soul towards themselves. The soul must first make intense effort to resist the pull of the world, and assert God's pull. When the attraction to the world is sufficiently reduced, the soul will be pulled towards God without a conscious effort of its own.

As light shines in a bulb, we can *speak* of light *in* the bulb but the bulb cannot imprison light. Light reflected in the bulb *can imagine it is imprisioned*. That is your condition. You are a divine light thinking that you are a physical body. Souls can become ignorant of their true being. That has happened to you. You are ignorant of your true identity that is God-like and you are living a sorrow frought life, identified with the mortal and imperfect body with the delusion, "I am a mortal person, qualified by a name, form, age, sex etc." The same soul, an immortal part of God, in-dwelling in different bodies, in different births, identifying with them, functions and lives as different persons, identified with a name, form, age, and sex which are qualified by the life lived as a person. The soul is not qualified by name and form. It is above name and form.

There are no good souls and bad souls. Heaven and heavenly beings can never be other than Perfect and you as a soul are a heavenly being. There are only perfect but ignorant and deluded souls involved by God, in good and bad lives, and thereby being educated. Those souls, who are conscious of their true identity, but are unidentified with persons while living as persons, are *free*. Wisdom to enable bound souls to become free is what is stated in this exposition.

You are a *Jivatma-individual conscious being*

The Vedantic name for your true Self is *'Atman'*. *Atman* means what you really are and not what you think you are. You think you are a living being or a *jiva* but really you are an individual conscious being or *Jivatma* and God is the Cosmic Being or *Paramatma*. You think you are a living being and your entire life is lived from that wrong belief. A story will illustrate this.

Mr. Bhargav was a happy bachelor who was fifty years old. One morning a young man who looked like a foreigner stepped into his room. "Am I speaking to Mr. Bhargav?" he asked. When Bhargav nodded his head in affirmation, the young man spoke as follows: "Sir, thirty years ago, you were in Paris, as a student in the Sorbonne University. You had a love affair there with a student named Mademoiselle Madeline. You left her without marrying her. I am her son, your son. She never told me about you until two months ago. Two months ago she died, but before she died, she told me about you, and gave me your address, and photograph. After her demise, I found myself in great difficulty, and what is more natural than for a son in distress to come to his father for protection. So I have come to you."

Hearing this, Bhargav was stunned to say the least. Soon he recovered himself, and being a person of integrity, said, "Stay with me, I will look after you." The young man did so and proved to be an utterly unworthy fellow, lazy, and dissolute. Poor Bhargav lost all his peace of mind and gaiety. His heart was heavy. Eighteen months passed, since he said goodbye to happiness.

One night, a Mr. X, an old and trusted friend of Bhargav, came to him and after carefully closing the door, he whispered, "Is your son here?" Bhargav answered with a heavy heart, "No, his usual time for returning at night is after midnight, never before." Assured of the young man's absence, Mr. X spoke as follows, "Dear Bhargav I have good news for you. The young French man, who is here pretending to be your son, is merely a pretender and an imposter, and not your son. From the very beginning, I doubted the fellow's words. He does not look in the least like you, but that is no proof that he is not your son. I have a son-in-law studying in Paris, however, and I wrote to him six months ago, giving him the details of this fellow and asking him to go to the Surete, the French police, and institute inquiries. His reply came last night. This fellow is not your son. It is true that Madeline was your girl friend but she had no son, by you or by anyone else. She remained true to your memory and did not marry. This young man wormed his way into her confidence, learned about you before her death, and has played this drama to live at your expense."

Bhargav was amazed, and asked searching questions and examined the letters from Paris, establishing beyond a shadow of doubt, the duplicity of the young man. The moment the conviction 'he is not my son' dawned on him all his sorrow vanished like mist before the morning sun. The long banished happiness rushed into him. In a few minutes he looked ten years younger. Mr. X took his leave, profusely thanked by him.

The next morning, after breakfast, Bhargav called the young fellow and said the following. "I have corresponded with the police in Paris and have ascertained that you are an imposter." The young man turned pale, and shook with fear. Bhargav continued "Do not be afraid, I am not going to prosecute you, or even eject you. My goodwill for you remains, but my personal attachment for you due to my delusion for you is gone. You are free to stay here if you wish and try to mend your ways. I shall help you to rehabilitate yourself." The young man left without a word and was not seen in the house for two days. On the third day, he came to Bhargav touched his feet, asked for forgiveness, and then returned to France.

Dear reader, realize that the mortal imperfect body is not your real identity. You are really an immortal and perfect God-like Being. The moment you achieve an intellectual conviction by understanding the truth, you will be greatly relieved from all sorts of sorrows. When your conviction becomes experience, all your sorrow will be gone lock, stock, and barrel.

You are God-Like and Heir to All that God is

You, as a soul are really a God-like Being. What God *is* that you also, *are*. God is all pervading. You are also all pervading because you resemble God. As God is Perfect, so as a soul you also are, even now, but you do not know it. God cannot be known as an object, and you cannot know yourself as an object. You can only experience yourself. God is not in the world. The world is in Him because the world is God's thought. What you really are is not in the world. Where God is, there you also are. Only what you think you are is in the world, the body-mind complex. When your knowing is corrected, your thinking also will be corrected and you will know the truth about your true identity. When you know the truth about yourself, you will know that the world is within you.

God, your Eternal Father, knows all, can do what He wants, never suffers, never is disturbed, never is anxious, never feels defedent, nor inadequate. As He is, you can be because as an *Isvara Putra*, you inherit His likeness. And what is more, He wants to make you as He is.

Let me put it this way. There were two celestial singers. They were like gods of music. They became mortal because of an order by God with a purpose. One was posed with high musical knowledge, and the other was mediocre in music. Functionally, the different potency of the singing capacity of the two musicians is important but intrinsically it does not matter. Why? Because in truth they are celestial singers and their real musical ability is in a quite different dimension or higher dimension. Therefore the good and average capacity of the two singers as mortal persons does not matter. So too, you should remember that the functional differences of each one of you is due to different potencies of your physical and mental qualities. But in truth, all human beings are

*Isvara Putra*s, heir to a different range and type of knowledge, thought, and action than the present human ones. To want it with all your heart, mind, strength, and soul is your duty. The rest is God's.

You are Connected to Your Body

You, a God-like Being are related or connected to your body, but you are really distinct from it. Spiritual progress consists in increasing in the meaningfulness of this sentence to you. I say you are only related to your body, and not really your body. By body I mean all the three bodies: namely the physical body, the mental body, and the causal body. Ignorance is the causal body. To put it differently, by body I mean, all that is now *known* as your self. Your physical body and your thoughts are known to you, therefore, it is not you because the knower cannot be the known. To put it still in another way, you are only living with the instruments of action, instruments of cognition, and the mind or the inner instrument. But you are not the instruments.

Gross people require the activities of the instruments of action to be happy. Finer people can be happy exercising their instruments of cognition. Still finer people can be happy exercising their minds alone. People who can be happy exercising their minds for the inquiry into the Self are the finest. A spiritual practitioner should live with the mortal body in such a way as to know that he or she is really an immortal being.

You are Essentially a Knower but Misknow What You Know

You are a walker, talker, eater, breather, thinker etc but essentially you are a knower. Knowing is your subtlest function. Only consciousness can know and you are a knowing consciousness.

God is also a knower: both you and God are knowers. But He is the Great Knower without defects in His cognition, and you are a small knower with defective cognition. God knows the world as His form and the activities of the world as His play. He knows the world as a *sadhana kshetra*, a place for culturing or preparing souls to enter Heaven but you misknow the world as a *bhoga kshetra*, a place of enjoyment. You misknow your life as your own life, and misknow your body as your own self. That is the problem.

God, the Great Knower is always behind you, the small knower, sustaining, and evolving your knowing consciousness, which is deluded now, till you attain God-like-Knowing, and God-like-Being. Therefore, your first task in spiritual life is to correct your present knowing of all that you know. In other words, you should correct your misknowing with the true knowing by practicing the right awareness of the five truths. When the misknowing is replaced by true knowing, you will experience that you are different from the known. Now, though we all know the logic that the knower is different from the known, we do not care about it. We accept the logic but it does not work in our lives. We do not live the truth because we don't know that we have a defect in our knowing. This is a spiritual disease.

Your State after Liberation

To distinguish yourself from a God-played role, as an *Isvara Putra*, an immortal soul is to be liberated. After liberation you experience yourself as a Witness of God's play. You will experience the activities of the ego taking place without any effort on your part, in your knowing consciousness as so many other activities like breathing, heart beats, blood circulation, digestion, and dreaming are now taking place without any effort on your part. Let me illustrate this with a story.

There was an actor named   Raj. He used to play different roles like Gandhi, Hamlet etc but he was not a talented actor and he did not make much money. One day in dream he found a middle age man speaking to him. The man said, "O Raj, know that I am Gautam. I was an actor like you. I died sixty years ago. I was a great actor but the jealous society did not recognize my talent and I died in obscurity. I have unsatisfied ambitions. Allow me to enter into you when you step onto the stage from the green room. I will play the role that you have to perform. I do not want anything from you except an opportunity to express my suppressed talents. You will take all of the credit and I will do all the work. Raj did so. All the people were astonished. The critics raved about him. He became very rich and was judged to be the greatest actor of his time.

Now I tell you, " As Raj was only a witness of Gautam's acting, having nothing to do with it really though people thought that he was doing it, so will you be after liberation – an uninvolved spectator of God's maskrade or *Isvara Lila* enacted in your witnessing consciousness.

In fact you are not at all involved in life but due to defective cognition, you think you are. Let me explain. A father and his son are sitting on a riverbank. The river is rising fast. The son is staring at his reflection in the water. Suddenly he forgets where he is (safe, besides his father on riverbank) and he thinks that he is in the waters, drowning. He cries for help. The father pinches his shoulder and the son comes to his senses and realizes that he was never in the water at all. Similarly, you should understand that you are not at all involved in life but due to defective cognition you think you are and undergoing various experiences. What is your duty after understanding this? You must seek your Self-Realization as your great goal of life and make your earthly life a means to it.

Accept Your Connection with Your Body and Live Wisely With It

A leech is a lizard-like insect, which likes to drink blood through the skin and it is almost impossible to remove it by force, until it is satisfied. I imagine a doctor putting a special leech on a boy's body saying, "Till this leech has drunk all your bad blood, you cannot remove it. When it has drunk all your bad blood, it will itself leave you. If you want the leech to leave you quickly, do not eat impure food." Similarly, your body is like a leech that God has put onto you, a soul, and it won't leave you, until your ignorance is fully gone. So your connection with the body must be accepted and used wisely to realize your *Isvara Putra* Self. Why is suicide is bad? It is because it is an attempt to terminate the connection with the body before Self-Realization.

Because you don't know the glory of the soul, you are able to tolerate the body. To one who knows the glory of the soul, the body is an unwanted adjunct. You are not the adjunct: you shine through the adjunct. Activities performed through the adjunct do not qualify you. It is like the case that your voice sounding through a bad microphone is actually not your voice. So, accept your connection with your body, live wisely, and experience your eternal connection with God. Your connection with the body changes with every birth. Your connection with the world continues till liberation but it also has an end; it is not permanent. Your connection with God, the Great Player is not endable: it is Eternal.

Understand the Truth Pertaining to Your Body

Your Body is God's Mask

Your physical body, which you now think of as you, is really God's mask wearing which He plays His play. The physical body is the outer mask and the mind is the inner mask. The word mask should remind you that it is God's mask. In Sanskrit a mask is called *Vesham*, and the Lord is called *Isvara*. Therefore the words *Isvara Vesham* means the mask of the Lord.

Your Body is a Part of Creation

Your body is a part of creation and is constructed by God. It is a creative construction of God. It is ever changing, compounded of elements, mortal and imperfect.

You Act through Your Body

Your physical body is an instrument through which you, the soul, an *Isvara Putra* do your activities. The physical body is your outer instrument and the intellect is your inner instrument through which you act and think.

Various Classifications of the Body According to Vedanta and Buddha

The physical body which is maintained by the intake of air, water, food, and warmth and which is left behind at death, is called the physical sheath or *annamaya kosa* in Vedanta and *rupaskanda* by Buddha.

The five organs of action that make walking, taking, speaking, excretion, and procreation possible are the organs of action and they are called *karmendriyas*. The organs of action do not refer to the physical legs, hands etc but to subtler organs within them. This is vedantic teaching. The respiratory system or the subtle faculty behind the breathing process is the vital sheath and it is called *pranamaya kosa*.

The five faculties of sense perception namely seeing, hearing, smelling, tasting, and tactile sensation, are the organs of knowledge or the sense organs and they are called *gnanendriyas*. Again the organs of knowledge do not refer to the physical eye, ear, etc but to subtler organs within them. The two functions associated with the sense organs are sensation and perception. Sensations are said by Buddha to belong to *vedana skandha*, and perceptions are to belong to *sanna skandha*.

In general the mind is called the inner instrument or antahkarana. The inner instrument has four functions; that which thinks with vacillation is called *manas*, that which inquires and makes decisions is called *buddhi*, the memory is called *chitta* and the egoism is called *ahankara*. Buddha calls mental activity *sanskara skandha* and Vedanta calls it *manomaya kosa*. The, faculty of being conscious of inner and outer things is called *vinnana* by Buddha, and he refers to it as *vinnana skandha*. The Vedanta refers to it as *vignanamaya kosa*. In the Vedanta the State of unconsciousness in deep dreamless sleep, accompanied by happiness is called the *anandamaya kosa*. Thus there are five sheaths or *kosas* and five skandhas.

The Vedanta classifies the five sheaths under three bodies and three states. The three bodies are: (1) the gross body, which constitutes the physical sheath o r *annamaya kosa*, (2) the subtle body which constitutes the vital sheath or prana, and also *mano,* and *vignanamaya kosas*, and (3) the causal body that stands for the sheath of bliss or *anandamaya kosa*.

The three states are the states of wakefulness, the state of dreaming, and the state of dreamless sleep.

Removal of the Causal Body is Liberation

Both the outer and the inner body are constructed and played by God and by itself are insentient. Though they should be discarded to experience our true identity, they are good for us now as they enable us to be conscious. Without it we would not be able to see, hear, breathe, or think. It would be unwise however, to forget its true function for us, and to regard it as ourselves, and live with it for itself. This is what most of us do, and this is what is responsible for all the misery and confusion in the world. When we understand the true significance of the subtle and gross bodies that we are conjoined with, and live with them rightly for the dissociation and removal of the causal body, then, and then only are we living wisely.

When the physical body dies, the subtle body and the causal body survive; they exist on another plane of existence for awhile, and then they reenter the world with another physical body. The purpose of God in connecting you, an *Isvara Putra*, with a physical body is to do away with your causal body. Until the causal body is fully gone, the subtle body will take rebirth. When the causal body is gone, the subtle body will not take rebirth after physical death and it will merge into subtle cosmic elements.

What exactly the causal body is, how it came to be, and why it should be removed, we will go into subsequently. The causal body stands for the nescience or spiritual ignorance or *agnana* that has enveloped the soul, obliterated its consciousness, and subjected it to a total oblivion. In beginningless time, the soul was obscured by ignorance, and unconscious and inert. God conjoined the soul with the subtle and gross bodies of His making. The causal body and the souls both existed from the very beginning. They were not made or created by

God. Ignorance was the occasion for God to make the subtle and gross bodies. He conjoined the souls with them to remove its/their ignorance. If the souls were not covered with ignorance God would have had no occasion to make the subtle and gross bodies. Therefore, ignorance constitutes the occasional cause or conditional cause for God to make the subtle and gross bodies, and, therefore the ignorance is called the causal body.

The causal body thus is like the disease of the soul, the disease of being subject to *becoming*, due to the loss of the knowledge of one's true *Being*. The subtle and gross bodies are like inner and outer medicines. The life in the world is the treatment for the disease, administered by the greatest of all doctors, *Vaidyanathan*. (Vaidyanathan is one of the names of Lord Siva meaning the Lord of medicine, and it also the author's name). Therefore, understand that your body is really God's mask or *Isvara Vesham*, and live with it wisely to experience your immortal soul.

Understand the Truth Pertaining to your Person

Your Person is a Role Played by God

The one who thinks, "I am the body" and works through the body and appropriate the activities of the body as, "my life", is the person. The person is the apparent user of the body or mask therefore, I call the person a *maskrader* meaning the user of the mask.

The person is a dramatic role played by God. In that sense, each one of us (as person) is a dramatic role played by God. In truth, all living creatures including the insects, the birds, the animals and man, from the worst sinners to the greatest saints, are all roles played by God. In Sanskrit, a dramatic role is called *nataka patram*. So, *Isvara Nataka Patram* means God's dramatic role.

In another way of speaking, the person is an 'I am so and so' mental mode of God. The ego is the 'I am so and so' thought. It is the first thought or first mental mode through which God plays His various roles. In Sanskrit the mental mode is called *bhava* or *ahambhava*. Therefore, a person can be equated to the ego or *ahamkara*. The ego stands for the bio-mental nature, which we express in every thing that we do.

Yet in another way of speaking the mortal person is the one who is born, grows, develops, dies, and then is reborn. Therefore, the person can also be equated to the *jiva*, which means a living being. A living, breathing person is jiva.

The words person, ego, *maskrader*, apparent self, everyday self, *jiva*, *bhava*, *jiva bhava*, *ahambhava*, *ahamkara*, dramatic role of God, *Isvara Nataka patram*, are equivalent.

Your Person Is Played By God for Your Ultimate Good

The condition of the souls is the occasion for God to play the role that He is playing. For example, a birthday is an occasion for us to be gay. Death is an occasion for people to mourn. Similarly the ignorance and the subsequent deluded condition of the souls in their evolution to their goal is the occasion for God to play the kind of roles that He is playing. Some souls are in such a condition that God has to play "bad roles." Some souls are in such a condition that God sees fit to play noble roles. The One God is playing so many roles for the sake of the ultimate good of the souls, the *Isvara Putra*s.

You Are Identifying Yourself With the Person

I do not think that any normal person has a problem in identifying himself. We all identify ourselves with our bodies. Though we do not make the act of identification with the body consciously, our behavior manifests that identification. All of us act according to our nature and in acting in accordance with that nature, we manifest identification with the body. We are all governed by a person-nature so to speak, which differs in some aspects in each of us but which we all have. Person-nature makes us act to identify ourselves with the body, and sometimes to distinguish ourselves from it.

Persons differ widely in their physical features and their natures. Thus we can speak of a role-nature or a person-nature as operative in all persons, but we have differences. All persons are born, grow, breathe, experience hunger and thirst, derive satisfaction, and die. We, the *Isvara Putra*s are identifying with the person-nature and we experience hunger, thirst, old age etc.

When we first see a man, we identify him by his form, dress, and other features like his voice. The more we get to know him, it is his 'character' which we apprehend as "him." What is it that we apprehend when we remember Krishna or Abraham or Hamlet? It is their character. In that way, we, that is, what we think we are, are essentially characters on the stage of life. We seem to live a life but we are really 'characters' played by God. Every ego is a character. No character is static. Characters not only express themselves but they change and they evolve. Sinners who become saints are dramatic instances, but in less obvious ways all characters are always in a process of evolution.

There is nothing wrong with the ego, as long as it is remembered that it is only a dramatic role played by God and not our true identity. There is no harm in identifying ourselves with our egos. The problem comes only when there is delusion in that identification.

Wanting to fulfill oneself as a Person is Wrong

We find our identity in the body and attempt to fulfill ourselves in a life of relationship with others. It is like a person deriving satisfaction from having in his room a number of statues and photographs of himself. We feel 'I am' and to know what we are, we utilize the body and the environment, as a field of self-expression and self-fulfillment. But we do not have to identify with the body to fulfill our selves and it is in truth not possible because we are not the body. We only act through the body. We are conscious beings, independent of the body.

If we examine our relationship with the body with which we are so intimately associated, we shall discover that sometimes we 'I' it thus identifying with it, and sometimes we 'my' it, thus distinguishing ourselves from it. This shows that we now have a confused idea of ourselves, though we don't care about it. Some of us might have strongly felt our distinctness from the body but we are not clear about what we are exactly, and we are content to jog along without feeling impelled to seek a clear answer. Also even after learning that we are not the body or the ego, we cannot end this identification. This does not mean however, that we can do nothing about it. According to Higher Wisdom, it is of the utmost importance that we seek and obtain a clear answer to the question of exactly how we are different from the person. Further Higher Wisdom says that there is no greater good than knowing our true identity.

I invite you to make the attempt and I give you all the necessary advice and inducement through this exposition.

Understand the Truth Pertaining to Your Life

Your life is God's Play and Purpose Oriented

I say, your life is God's divine play or *maskrade* or *Isvara Lila* because God has no personal lack to fulfil through the play and He plays effortlessly, gracefully, and beautifully without any selfish motive.

There is no purpose to children's play, except the playing of it. What is the purpose of laughter? Has laughter any purpose? It is merely the spontaneous expression of happiness. A sport is generally purpose-less. God's divine sport is not purposeless in that sense but it is purpose oriented. The purpose is dual, and they are the liberation of the individuals, and the evolution of the world. Let me explain the significance of God's divine play like this. A boy has slipped and fallen into a ditch and he comes to the father covered with dirt. The father instead of removing the unwanted matter, which is dirt, further adds other extraneous matters like soap and water. Then he rubs causing pain to the body. Finally he pours a lot of nice warm water, and the boy is clean.

The pure body of the boy is the soul of human beings. The dirt on the boy's body is beginning-less ignorance. The soap is the outer or gross creation and the water mixed with soap is the inner or subtle creation. In short, God's divine play is like the soap and water, the physical body is like that of the soap, and our thoughts are like the soap mixed with water. The vicissitudes of life and the experiences of pain and pleasure that we have to undergo are like the rubbing of the soap and water by the father on his son. The Grace of God finally descending upon the soul, washing away all ignorance and erroneous cognition is like the final rinsing of the boy with pure warm water so that all the dirt is completely loosened and not clinging. The rubbing is God's lawful governing and the rinsing is His Grace. While the father is rubbing roughly in places where the dirt is clinging, the boy cries and protests and resists. The soul that complains and blames God is like this. When the boy finally understands the loving intentions of his father behind the rough treatment, he becomes quiet and the rubbing take place much less painfully.

Love promotes understanding. There are limits to many things but there is no limit to love. Love is Infinite. Understand that Infinite Love is behind this suffering world. Through earthly attachments, the inert soul is being evolved. God causes, permits, and encourages earthly attachments for the development of the soul. He also breaks them when necessary for the evolution of the soul. You give the baby a nipple to suck. You also take it away and the baby cries. Still you take it away.

Primordial ignorance of your true identity is a disease. God's divine play is like medicine: God is the doctor, life is treatment, the world is a hospital, discharge from the hospital is liberation, arriving home whole and healthy is the non-dual At-one-ment with God and the Knowledge of RA, the Substratum Self.

Divine Play Takes Place According to the Law of God

The order in which the divine play takes place is the Law of God. By the Law of God I mean the laws of material and moral causation. The Law of God is called *Isvara Niyati* in Sanskrit. *Isvara* means the Lord and *Niyati* means order.

The world is God governed and God is the sole Governor of it. Not only results but the nature of the endeavors you make to attain results are also governed by the Laws of God. There is no incident that is not ruled by the Laws of God's government. Nothing can happen outside it. Even the exercise of free will takes place in the orbit of the Laws of God. I will explain this later more fully. People believe that everything happens according to fate, but this is not a precise and a proper way of stating the truth. Law of God controls everything, even the way you choose. However, God does not wish that there should be a train accident on such and such a day. God has no 'will' as people think. God's 'Will' is only good will that operates through His order. Every happening is God's play and the play takes place according to His Law. God's Law does not grant freedom of choice to animals but grants it to human beings.

The Law of God's government takes place according to your actions or *karma*. Knowing your life as God's divine play is only a sweet way of recognizing the influence of your past activities over your present behavior.

Divine Play is Education for Your Awakening

From the point of view of divine sport, all is God's perfect *acting*. Buddha's attaining Nirvana is God's divine play. Hitler's massacre of the Jews was God's divine play. The perfect acting of God is in both cases. There are not good and bad activities from the point of view of God's divine play. All the activities are perfect as God's *acting*. There are no grades in God's acting. But God's play takes place *through your free will*. So, from the mundane point of view, there are good acts and bad acts and you are responsible for your choices, Throughout your life you make choices. You choose those things that you think are good for you but most of the time you are not right. For example sometimes what you once thought was good is found not to be good latter. The divine play is educating you to discriminate between the good and the bad to enable you to realize what is not good, and what is good for you. Life is educating you regarding values. What you think, "it is good for me" is a value. The finer the values, the finer and subtler the mind. The education reaches its final stage when you aspire for the highest of all values and become indifferent to, or more or less choiceless, regarding other lesser values.

Through attachments to sons, daughters, friends, mother, relatives, your guru, your country etc, you develop. The wise one is conscious of these truths and goes wisely and smilingly through the lives of attachments and finally attains everlasting Peace. The drama of bondage and liberation can only be enacted in a transparent mind. In a highly transparent mind the drama reaches its denouncement of liberation.

Divine Play is Factual but not Reality

The criteria for differentiating between fact or *mithya* and Truth or *satya* are this. Whatever has a beginning and an ending, however long the interval is between the two - whether a few seconds or aeons, is fact and whatever has no beginning and no end but always is, is Truth.

Existence is factual, but it is not Reality. What exists is fact. Facts are known through the mind or inner instrument. Whatever is known is impermanent, unreal, and subject to the duality of pain and pleasure. With the help of the mind we (must) try to have knowledge which corresponds to the fact. This is what scientists do. They try for knowledge, which corresponds to the facts of the outer world. But Truth cannot be known through the mind. Facts are known but they change; therefore they are not Truth. God's divine play changes, therefore it is not Truth. But it cannot exist apart from the Truth or Reality. The unreal cannot exist apart from Reality. The unreal is the Real appearing so. The world that we experience through our senses is a stream of effects issuing from a source, which is God. When we see a fountain spouting from a source, we see an apparently steady column of water, but we know that the steadiness is only an appearance, and what actually is, is a quickly changing succession of water drops. A river appears to be the same at different times, but actually waters are always filing past, and the same water does not exist at any point, but different water takes its place. So too, God's divine sport is like a river in that it is a stream of effect issuing from God, and constant unceasing change characterizes it. The appearance has continuity but the actuality is in constant change. Therefore it is not really real. Our lives too are part of God's divine play. They begin with birth and end with death, and therefore they are fact and unreal. But while God's divine play is unreal, God is Real. He is Eternal, Truth, and Bliss. We as persons are facts and unreal but we as *Isvara Putra*s and God are the same kind and Eternal.

Truth Does Not Cancel Your Responsibility

It has been said that your life or all activities are God's *maskrade* or *Isvara Lila*. This means that the thief thieving is God's *maskrade*, the judge punishing him is God's *maskrade* and the judge punishing the thief wrongly is also God's *maskrade*. Good action, and bad action, careful action, and careless action, lying, and cheating, speaking the truth, and acting justly are all God's *maskrade* as are sinning, repenting and living a reformed life afterwards.

Hearing this one might say, "What is the use of this teaching that all acts are God's *maskrade*? Then everyone can do what he likes and call it God's *maskrade*, and say we are not responsible for what we do. If we fail in our exam it is not our fault. God played it so. Terrorist killings are God's *maskrade*. So no one is to blame." Also one may say, "When people misbehave, we should not be angry or hurt because it is only God's play and the play is unreal. Then if people are kind and good that is also God's play, and therefore unreal so we should not smile or be pleased. Is that right? If everything is God's play and unreal, what should we try for?"

Let me answer. Yes, everyone can do what he likes and call it God's *maskrade*. For example, if your sister spills ink on your clothes saying it is God's *maskrade*, you will give her a slap saying this is also God's *maskrade*. Is that not so? So what does it show? Though, there is nothing that anyone can do anywhere at any time that is not God's play, the play is enacted via your freewill. You should understand that the play is taking place through your free will, which though it is limited, it is there and for that limit, and within that limit you are responsible. We all have a certain amount of free will which we are exercising constantly whether we know it or not. For example, adults are responsible for their actions but small children are not responsible for the 'wrongs' that they may do. When they grow up or mature we hold them responsible for their acts, and they become liable for blame when they do wrong. Similarly, now you have come of age. You should understand the truth of things and accept your responsibility.

An amateur game is not played for money or for egoism. It is played for the pleasure of playing the game fairly and efficiently. One should take defeat and victory lightly and sportly. Similarly we should try to achieve an auspicious life and a righteous society but we should be conscious that it is only a game that we are playing for Self-Realization and take the ups and downs lightly. The playful spirit (not flippant spirit) trying for worthwhile things is what is wanted. The world is a place where we are being tranced or deluded to attain an equal mind with regard to the ups and downs of life. So the world is a place designed to upset you and you must learn not to be upset. Play your life or play your part with God in righteousness with the spirit of serving God and be a responsible co-player with Him but do not make an anxious burden of it.

Accept God's Government with Love and Respect

Whatever has a beginning will have an ending. This is the law of life. Childhood will have to be given up to experience boyhood and girlhood. Willy nilly, you will be forced to give up all that you are attached to, including your own person so, why not give up gracefully. Love the law of life. You will be happy and develop. The true scientist does not blame nature if his experiment fails. Trusting in the infallibility of nature is the foundation for a true scientist. To understand nature more and more and to benefit intelligently from that understanding is wisdom. Similarly, to understand God's Law better and better and to benefit intelligently from that understanding is wisdom. The one who complains against God's Law and has a grievance in regard to God's Law will not learn what it is meant to teach.

When I recognized this truth I thought that if individuals could be made to understand this truth, they would behave better. I thought that the individuals must be helped to understand that God has put them on earth to prepare them for entry into Heaven and by consciously cooperating with God they can enter Heaven more quickly. It is just as a doctor would say to a bad patient, "If you take the medicines at the proper time in the proper dose, and also observe the dietetic and other restrictions, *you will get cured more quickly.*"

Regarding your past misdeeds, repent, forget, and live anew. The order is repentance, regeneration, and reformation. The first two are an inner awakening and the last is an outer change.

Wise and Unwise View of Your Life

Every action of yours can be viewed from three ways, one being unwise and two being wise. Let me explain. Suppose a person, whom all know as Mr. A, did something. To know the action as "Mr. A did it", is unwise because Mr. A is only a dramatic role of God, and the role is not really real. Mr. A as we see is only a mask of God and the mask is insentient. The other two wise views are this: "a son of God, an *Isvara Putra* did it" in the condition of ignorance of his true identity and in the delusion of "I am Mr. A, and the other wise view is, "God 'played it" as Mr. A.

Good sons of God should cultivate both views because both are true. When you become a perfect son of God, then all of the actions done by Mr. A will be witnessed by you as an artistic play of God.

Do Not Identify yourself With the Play

Do not attach yourself with your life and claim it as yours because your life is God's play. But indifference is not the corrective for attachment; indifference is worse than attachment. Impersonal and objective goodwill for all or pure love is the best. I call pure love pure attachment, in distinction to emotional attachment. Emotional attachment is bad. Surrender your attachment to all your claims to God by knowing them as His play. Knowing your life as God's artistic play will loosen your attachment to the play and awaken you. When there is no inner attachment, outer actions will not bind you. Where there is inner attachment even though there is no outer action there is still bondage. The world is given to you, the son, as a means to know your Eternal Father, so use it, without being ensnared by it as a means to know your Eternal Father.

SECTION Q

Five Truths Pertaining to Others: Objective

Understand the Truth Pertaining to God with
        Regard to Others
Understand the Truth Pertaining to Others
Understand the Truth Pertaining to Their Body
Understand the Truth Pertaining to Their Person
Understand the Truth Pertaining to Their Life

The previous section emphasized the under-standing of the five truths with regards to oneself. This section emphasizes the understanding of the five truths with regard to every other human being. You incorporate the teachings of section P into this.

Understand the Truth Pertaining to God with Regard to Others

Understand that God is the Eternal Father of every individual. Understand that He is the Inner Ruler and Controller or *Antaryami* of everyone and also the Enlightener or *Guru* of every other individual whether they are young or old, sick or healthy, sinner or saint, good or bad or belong to this religion or to that religion etc. Understand that God is the Player of everybody's life and also the Witness of their lives.

Understand the Truth Pertaining to Others

Understand that others are also the offspring or sons of God or *Isvara Putra*s, including even the worst sinners, irrespective of their caste or their creed.

Understand the Truth Pertaining to Their Body

Understand that the physical body with, which you identify others as he and she is God's mask or *Isvara Vesham*. Understand that all, physical bodies are constructed by God and they belong to God. In fact all that is known is created by God and belongs to God.

Understand the Truth Pertaining to Their Person

Understand that every person or ego is a dramatic role played by God to awaken the concerned soul or *Isvara Putra*. What you think of him or her are really God's impersonational ego or maskrader or *Isvara Nataka Patram*, through which He plays His sport.

Understand the Truth Pertaining to Their Life

Understand that the lives of others are played by God to awaken them. Understand that the lives of everybody are God's play or maskrade or *Isvara Lila* and through their lives, God is awakening them to experience their true identity in their own direct experience. Understand that *this is the meaning of the life that they live*.

SECTION R

Understand that You Are Subjected to Defective Cognition and Therefore Living a Deluded Life

Your Problem is Defective Cognition

Though you are really an offspring of God, at present you do not have the experience of it. You have only the experience of yourself as your body and as a mortal person. This is due to your defective cognition. You have error in your knowing with regard to your person, your body, and your life, and therefore, you do not experience yourself as an offspring of God. Your self-consciousness is now in a confused condition due to defective cognition or *gnana dosham*; this defective cognition is your malady.

Defective Cognition is Due to Ignorance and Delusion

The cause of your defective cognition is your ignorance of your true identity, which in turn causes your subsequent delusion regarding your life. You are subjected to ignorance regarding the first two of the five truths, and you have a deluded identification regarding the last three. Because you do not have the experience of your true identity, you do not know God, and you also misknow what is God's as yours. But though you think that you are the body, in truth you are not the body. The body is an insentient known object but you are a conscious being. The body is known but you cannot know yourself as an object. You can only be yourself. Therefore, the idea that you are having now, about yourself as "I am a person" which underlies your entire existence, is a delusion. However this cannot in the least impair your real identity just as a person's daydream cannot affect the facts about him. What binds you is your thinking with defective cognition.

First Task is to Understand That You Are Living a Deluded Life

When your defective cognition is corrected, your delusion regarding all the known will be gone. When the delusion towards the known is completely gone, your ignorance will evanesce. When the ignorance is gone, the truth will dawn. So, the first thing to do is to understand that you are living a deluded life and therefore having a defective cognition regarding all that you know. You should be clear about this in your mind.

Where there is suffering, know that there is delusion. When an actor, Mr. A, plays a role on the stage, he does not suffer because he knows who he really is and he knows the truth about the play. The played role cannot suffer because it is only an imagined mental mode in the mind of Mr. A. It is not really real. Similarly when God impersonates as 'I am so and so,' God, the Player, does not suffer because He knows the truth about Himself and His play. The 'played I', that is the ego, cannot suffer because the ego is only a mode or the prime thought played by God and it is not really real. But there is suffering and it is obvious that you are the sufferer. Why do you suffer, why do you undergo the experiences of pain and pleasure instead of being in Bliss and in Peace? It is because you identify yourself with the ego with delusion and therefore you think that you are a person. Because of your deluded identification with the person, you have defective cognition and you suffer. So, your first task is to understand that you are now living a deluded life with defective cognition, and you must work for its removal.

SECTION S

Understand that Your Deluded Life is the Therapy for Your Ignorance or Agnana.

Meaning of Life

Your ignorance of your true identity is beginningless but your identification with the body as 'I am so and so' has a beginning and it has been caused by God for your good. You are involved in life by God without your conscious knowing of it. So, though your deluded identification is an evil from one point of view, it is really a Grace of God in disguise. Under the benign direction of God, your delusion is functioning as a remedy for your beginningless malady, which is your ignorance of your true identity.

Your deluded condition is the reason for God to play the kind of role He is playing. Through your deluded identification with the body, God is removing your delusion in your knowing. Innumerable are the lives, that you have lived previous to this, conjoined with innumerable bodies, human and subhuman, and in all of them, God has been inseparably present with you as your Inner Ruler and Controller, evolving you, erasing more and more of your ignorance of the truth about yourself. Understand that you are living in God's play, educated by God's play, and being evolved through God's play to experience your ever-attained true Self. *This is the meaning of the life that you live.*

I said that mere identification with the body is not the problem but deluded identification is the problem. So, first you should become a knower without delusion.

World is A Soul Awakening Theatre

In a hospital you will hear shrieks and other horrible sounds but you know that good doctors are treating sick patients and the place is not a torture chamber. Even so the world appears like a torture chamber but understand that it is a soul awakening theatre. There is no suffering that living beings undergo which is not a medical treatment for their defective cognition.

Life is a Therapy for Defective Cognition

You see all around you people living a variety of lives, both good and bad. The variety of good and bad is due to the varying degrees of the state of defective cognition of the various souls or *Isvara Putra*s. There are many kinds of defective cognition and God is playing many kinds of roles that are related to the defective cognition of the concerned *Isvara Putra*s. There are so many kinds of lives - fortunate, unfortunate, prosperous, poor, healthy, unhealthy etc. but all are therapies for the defective cognition of *Isvara Putra*s. The liberated ones whom I call perfect sons of God see all the happenings in the world as soul awakening therapy. The good sons of God should practice seeing the happenings in that way.

Understand that God will not allow you to find rest in His dramatic roles or maskraders, because He loves you. *This is the meaning behind the mystery.*

I Grant Your Point

Now you may ask, "Cannot the Great, All Knowing, All Able, All Loving, All Wise God effect His therapy with less suffering?" If you ask, I grant you your point but I have no answer. I will not defend Him. I have no answer.

SECTION T

Understand that God Requires Your Cooperation

This section says that God requires your Conscious Cooperation to facilitate and expedite the fulfillment of His intention for you, which is to reveal to you in your own direct experience your true identity. Also it says that even now, in your present condition of deluded cognition, you are serving God, though inefficiently, and unconscious-ly.

Cooperative Living is Your Obligation and Privilege

It has been said that you are an immortal soul being evolved through the life that you live to know the glorious truth about yourself, and that the Creator requires your Conscious Cooperation. Now the question, "Are we free?" will never arise to the common man because he is experiencing his freedom every second. We experience freedom. Also, even if one can see that the experience of freedom is an illusion or a delusion, one cannot deny the experience. Sri Krishna's saying to Arjuna at the end of his discourse in the Gita, "I have told you. Now act as you think fit," proves it.

That we are free is as true as that we are, governed by God. God's government and freedom of choice are not incompatible. Freedom is the condition for development. Freedom implies the liability to err. Error is the price of freedom, and development is the prize of freedom. But development requires the right exercise of freedom. Choosing for God is the right way of exercising your (God-given) freedom. I call this Pro-God living.

God is intimately associated with you, sharing the life that you live and He requires your conscious choosing for Him to enable Him to bestow upon you, His likeness. To this purpose, He has involved you in the creation. Among the creatures, human beings are the only one who can understand this and cooperate with the Creator's design for him through him, for all concerned. So, to offer your Conscious Cooperation to the Great Player is both your obligation and your privilege.

Even Now, You Are an Unconscious Server of God

I have said that God requires your Conscious Cooperation to facilitate and expedite the fulfillment of His intention for you. Now I say, whether you accept it or not, you are a server of God even now and serving His world, by the manner of your living, though unconsciously, and evolving the world for the good or for the worst.

The world that you live in owned in every bit by God. The body that you live with is made, maintained, and owned in every bit by God. The breath by which you breathe and live is His. Your 'free will' is His gift. Being so completely dependent upon Him, what is the idea of being independent and living for your self? True, you think you are independent and living for yourself but all creatures (including yourself) are unknowingly, subserving the purpose of the Creator willy-nilly. While creatures are going about impelled by their desires and seeking their own gratification, the Creator's purpose through them, for them, and for all concerned is being advanced. Let me give you a few examples.

The greyhound chasing an electric hare in the racecourses of the west does not know that he is serving his master when he wins a prize by his swift running. He is only aware that there is a delicious edible in front of him, which ought to be grabbed and eaten; he is an unconscious server of his master's purpose.

In sexual congress, the ordinary man uses the woman for his gratification and vice versa, but nature uses both of them for each other and also for her continuance of the human race for history.

So, we do not have to do something special to affect the world; we are doing it by everything that we do. The humble housewife doing her chores in the kitchen, going to the grocer and to the temple, and living within the confines of a small area is also fashioning the natural, social, and cultural world condition. We have only to become conscious of the significance of our activities and perform them rightly in God's service. To understand and to accept your responsibility and adopt whatever changes that comes to your mind by that understanding is to consciously cooperate. Whoever seeks his liberation wisely will help the world progress, and whoever seeks to advance the welfare of the world will advance his own progress to liberation. Wise, however, is the man who is aware of both and lives balancing the claims of both, seeking no difference in them.

Here I would like to say this. My writings are not an invented fictitious theory to achieve good results, but an obligation derived from the truth of the constitution of the world and man's place in it for man to live cooperatively with God. If you look at the world keenly and do research on the constitution of man in history, that research will take you to this truth. Therefore, until the fundamental law that governs the world changes radically, my theory will not change, and cannot change, and therefore will never die.

Even if someone says that this theory will not be beneficial to humanity, even then I will not change it because truth is higher than good. Realistically speaking there can be no conflict between good and truth but because good is perceived mostly through ideas and is relative, in that sense, I put truth as higher than good.

Accept your *Isvara Putra* Self-hood and Live Cooperatively

If an individual accepts his or her *Isvara Putra* self-hood, then it follows that one should henceforth live as a conscious and cooperative son or daughter of God in God's play.

Conscious Cooperation is the axis of the practice for establishing the new way of life, which I have explained in four spiritual practices. It consists in the conscious living of the five truths and in making such revisions in one's actions and thoughts, as the new consciousness demands.

SECTION U

Cooperators are Called Good Sons of God or *Isvara Suputras*

Individuals who accept this philosophy, acknowledge themselves as offspring or sons of God, and try to live a conscious and cooperative life are called good sons of God or *Isvara Suputras.* I also call them conscious *Isvara Putra*s.

All human beings are related to God and are sons of God but not all know that they are related to God and are sons of God.

Those who either do not know that they are the offspring or sons of God, or even after knowing, are not interested in knowing their true identity and experiencing their non-dual At-one-ment with God and do not cooperate with Him, are ordinary sons of God.

Those who come to know that they are offspring or sons of God but now subjected to ignorance and delusion, and aspire to realize their true identity and cooperate with God are good sons of God.

Those who trouble the good sons of God are bad sons of God. Those good sons of God, who by cooperation have attained Self-Realization, are perfect sons of God.

The innate nature or *swadharma* of the perfect sons of God is to love the Creator, to desire the welfare of creation and to be always joyfully occupied in acts of service to creation. They teach the Higher Wisdom to others and motivate human beings to live as good sons of God. In other words they consciously cooperate with God.

Various Classifications of Isvara Putras

Offspring/son of God = *Isvara Putra*

Ordinary offspring/son of God = *Isvara Sadharana Putra*

Good offspring/son of God = *Isvara Suputra or Conscious Isvara Putra*

Bad offspring/son of God = *Isvara Kuputra*

Great offspring/son of God = *Isvara Uttama Putra*

Perfect offspring/son of God = *Isvara Sat Putra*

SECTION V

Cooperation Consists of Four Spiritual Practices

Conscious Cooperation with God is the 'way of life' I prescribe, and it consists of four spiritual practices: *sadhanas* A, B, C and D. A and B, are the *sadhanas* of Right Awareness of the Five Truths, subjective and objective. They are correctives for our cognitive defects. From the cognitive defects emotional and volitional defects arise. They are corrected through the *sadhanas* C and D, which deals with Righteous Living with a Service Spirit to God, subjective and objective. Right awareness of the five truths is the most important yet the most difficult to remember. I hope that this presentation will help ordinary people to remember and practice them.

A meditative attitude and the activities of life should go together. Let me give you an illustration. A woman came to a man and said, "I am a good secretary. I will assist you in every way. My parents are dead and I am alone. Please help me." The man engaged her as his personal assistance in all matters. Six months passed. The woman performed her work well, but her employer doubted her identity and wanted to find out her background. Another six months passed. The man was now living with the woman, still trying to find out who she really was. So too, you should live your life, and also try to know and realize the truth about yourself.

Your true Self, is action-less and thought-less, because it is Perfect and Blissful and it needs no action or thought to get anything. Even now, in your present deluded condition it is not lost, but only the experience of it is lost. To enable you to regain the experience of your true identity, God has made you an actor and a thinker having actions and thoughts. Though in truth God is the

Player of your life, He has made you experience that you are the author of your actions, and through that experience He is evolving you. So when the question is asked, "Who is acting and thinking?" the answer is you, the deluded soul or *Isvara Putra* with a defective cognition. You are responsible for your own activities and should revise them in the light of the new view of life. So, the first part of the spiritual practice is to Act Pro-God and Think Pro-God. The second part of the spiritual practice is to surrender your activities to God by reknowing your activities as played by God, and endeavor to be a Witness of your actions and thoughts. You should repeat the second part of the spiritual practice several times a day at a set time until it becomes natural to you. After realizing your true identity, which is the State of Witness, it will not be that you will be unable to think. What will happen is that your involuntary thinking, the thinking from your past tendencies will cease. Just as you speak only when necessary, you will also think *only* when necessary.

The ancient wise people said to humanity, "Understand the way of life that has been given to you by the wise. Earn your lively-hood according to that, enjoy the pleasures of life according to that, and if you do so it will take you to liberation." I prescribe the 'four spiritual practices' for your wellbeing, here and hereafter. Among them, the *righteous living with a service spirit to God, subjective and objective spells out the terms of the new life that is living for God.*

I feel like writing the following. I am not writing these words so much for this generation who are religiously orphaned, religiously bewildered, morally blind, and proud of their blindness. What will save the world, and make the world livable for the good, and the gentle, is the righteous living with the spirit of service to God. My writings are mainly to give man a tremendous inducement to do right from a Love of God, and to have a friendly feeling towards his fellow men.

WAY OF LIFE

Conscious and Cooperative Life with God, Consists of Four Spiritual Practices: *Sadhanas* A, B, C and D

SADHANA A

Right Awareness of the Five Truths Pertaining to You: Subjective

Be Conscious that God is Your Inner Ruler and Controller
Be Conscious that You are an Offspring or son of God or *Isvara Putra*
Be Conscious that God's Mask is Your Body
Be Conscious that God's Dramatic Role is Your Person
Be Conscious that God's Play is the Life You Live

Having sufficiently understood the five truths that were explained in the view of life, now those truths should be practiced and assimilated. The practice consists of four spiritual practices or *sadhanas* A, B, C and D that explain the method of conscious and cooperative way of life with God. They will help you to objectify your activities and ego and experience your non-dual Union or At-one-ment with God. *Sadhana* A speaks about the installation of the right awareness of the five truths regarding yourself correctly and firmly in your mind.

Be Conscious that God is Your Inner Ruler and Controller

Be always conscious that God is your Eternal Father and that He is ever present with you, as your Inner Ruler and Controller or *Antaryami*. He is both playing the life that you live and witnessing it. So, be conscious of Him as the Player of your life during your activities, and contemplate Him as the Witness of your thoughts during the meditation. Be conscious of God as your Eternal Father and Mother. Consider your earthly parents as His representatives. Remembering and cherishing the various aspects of God in relation to you as your Eternal Father, Eternal Guru, Divine Master, and Player and Witness of your life is the essence of this practice. Repeatedly studying and assimilating the teachings explained in the view of life will help you to establish the right awareness of the truth of God in relation to yourself.

The sacred words *Antaryami Pahimam*" meaning the Inner Ruler and Controller protect me, will remind you in this awareness.

Be Conscious that You are an Offspring or son of God or *Isvara Putra*

Be always aware of yourself as an offspring or son of God or *Isvara Putra*, wholly and solely, resembling Him and belonging to Him. The constant awareness that your true identity is not different from God, and even now in your present ignorant and deluded condition you do not cease to be that, is the essence of this second practice. Your ignorance has deprived you of the blissful experience of your filial relationship with God. But it has not and cannot deprive you of your true identity, which is not different from God. Your true identity cannot be loseable or even impairable, under any circumstances.

Keep reminding yourself now and then that you are an *Isvara Putra* until it becomes natural to you.

Be Conscious that God's Mask is Your Body

So far you had been thinking that you are your body and that it belongs to you. The third practice of *sadhana* A asks you to reknow your body as God's mask or *Isvara Vesham,* a property that belongs to God.

To reknow your body in this way is very difficult because you must remove all attachment to your own person. To objectify what you now regard, as your self is difficult. It is difficult to remove attachment to one's close kith and kin but it is even more difficult to remove attachment to one's own body. The repeated studying and digesting the view of life will reduce your I-ing and my-ing of the body. Along with the reknowing of your body as God's mask, you should also coplay your part with God in living your life.

You should not become indifferent to your body or to that of others. It is better to be attached than it is to be indifferent but it is best to be vitally concerned regarding your body and those of all others without attachment. It means, you should be interested in your body and those of others as the property of God. A story would illustrate this.

A young man went to a guru and asked to be accepted as his disciple. The guru said, "I will, accept you on the condition that you surrender your body to me." The young man said, "Done," whereupon the guru took a stick and tried to beat him. Instinctively the man raised his hands in defense. The guru said, "Is this surrender? Get out."

The next day the young man came again and said, "Sir your action was so sudden and unexpected that I failed. You test me now."

The guru took up the stick again and tried to beat him. Without defending himself the young man received many blows with a smile.

The guru said, "Is this surrender? Get out."

The guru's wife, who was watching this, said to her husband after the young man left, "Why were you angry with him. Did he not yield his body to be beaten by you without any mercy? What more do you want him to do?" The guru smiled and said, "Wait and see."

The next day the young man said, "Sir, you test me today *if you please*." The guru took up the stick and raised it to beat him. The young man raised both hands and warded off the blows as he had done on the first day.

The guru smiled and said, "Alright. You are my disciple. Go home and bring your belongings and come back." The young man rushed off joyfully.

The guru's wife who was watching all of this was much puzzled. She was wondering if her husband was joking or had lost his mind. She asked for an explanation. The guru replied, "The first day he defended his body considering it to be his own. The next day, he understood the body as *mine* but he *allowed it to be damaged*, by my blows. The third day, he understood the body as *mine* and he *defended it from damage*.

That is proper surrender." Reknowing the body as God's mask and treating it as belonging to God is the proper way of surrendering your body to God.

The sacred words 'God's mask' or '*Isvara Vesham*' will help you in the right awareness of you body.

Be Conscious that God's Dramatic Role is Your Person

The very awareness that your ego is a character played by God and that all of your mental activities are God's artistic expression, will enable you to rass your ego, meaning to look at it with an artistic delight. It will make you not to identify yourself with your ego and will allow you learn what you ought to learn to purify your mind.

The same person is known as father by one, grandfather by another, uncle by one, son by another, friend by one or enemy by another, and each person has different ideas about him related to their different modes of knowing. To know all persons including yourself, as a role that God is playing is a *revolutionary* though true knowing. The sacred word '*maskrader*' or '*Isvara Nataka Patram*' will enable you to establish in the right awareness of your person.

Be Conscious that God's Play is the Life You Live

To reknow your life as God's play is the fifth practice of this section. It is to be conscious that all that you think, feel, experience, speak, and do moment by moment in a continuous and uninterrupted succession in the course of your daily life at home, at office, and elsewhere, are enacted by God via your free will. But, you should never forget that the play is taking place according to your past actions or *karma* that stem forth from your own defective cognition. The awareness "my life is really God's play and it is educative" will make you not only objectify your entire life, but it will also make you live in righteousness and make right choices in your living. To make the right choice means to make a Pro God Choice. Always remember that when right awareness and cooperative living are operative, the delusion whose expression is the claiming of one's body and life as I and mine will be counteracted and attenuated. When the remembrance is not present, delusion will manifest unchecked. The awareness of your life as God's play will also make you not forget that the ultimate purpose of God's play is to awaken you from your primordial slumber and bestow upon you the experience of your true identity which is not different from God.

The sacred word *'maskrade'* or *'Isvara Lila'* will enable you to establish in the right awareness of your life.

SADHANA B

Right Awareness of the Five Truths Pertaining to Others: Objective

Be Conscious that God is Their Inner Ruler and
     Controller
Be Conscious that They are Offspring/sons of God
or *Isvara Putra*s
Be Conscious that God's Mask are Their Bodies
Be Conscious that God's Dramatic Roles are Their
     Persons
Be Conscious that God's Play are the Lives They
Live

Having established the awareness that has been told in Sadhana A, you need to follow it up by correcting your awareness of others. "As God is to me, so He is to everyone," is the essence of *sadhana* B.

In this practice you should attempt to distinguish the known part of others as God's play and try to be aware of the individual as God's offspring or *Isvara Putra*s. (This is not applicable to liberated souls). The revision of knowing others will correct your thoughts and actions regarding them. *This is the best way of pleasing and worshiping the Real Father of us all.*

Be Conscious that God is Their Inner Ruler and Controller

Just as God is your Eternal Father, He is also the Eternal Father of everybody else. As your Eternal Father is not dead because He is Immortal, and is behind your knowing consciousness, be conscious that God is the Eternal Father of everyone else, and that He is also behind the knowing consciousness, of them. As God is your Inner Ruler and Controller, He is the Inner Ruler and Controller of others also. As God plays your life to awaken you, He also plays the lives of everyone else to awaken them.

Be Conscious that They are Offspring or sons of God or *Isvara Putra*s

Just as you are an *Isvara Putra*, so others are also *Isvara Putra*s. As you belong to God, and resemble Him as an *Isvara Putra*, others also belong to God and resemble Him as *Isvara Putra*s. As you are now subjected to the ignorance of your *Isvara Putra self-hood* and deprived of the blissful experience of your true identity, they are also subjected to the ignorance of their *Isvara Putra self-hood* and thereby they are deprived of their blissful experience of their true identity.

Be Conscious that God's Masks are Their Bodies

To reknow the bodies of others as God's mask or *Isvara Vesham* is the third practice of this section. This is the right awareness of the physical body of others. It means that you should not give reality to the body but know it only as God's mask. At the same time you should be concerned with everybody because they belong to God, and you must serve everyone in such a way that God will be pleased by your service.

Be Conscious that God's Dramatic Roles are Their Persons

As your person or ego, is a mental mode of God, so all other persons are the mental modes of God and played by God. To reknow persons as God's dramatic roles or *maskraders* or *Isvara Nataka Patram* is the fourth practice of *Sadhana* B.

Be Conscious that God's Play are the Lives They Live

To reknow the lives of others as the play of God is the fifth practice of this section. This practice will remove all your negative thoughts towards them. This reknowing will help you to establish the true knowing of their lives. The expression of deluded knowing is the belief that all are really the body, and living your life according to that belief. The expression of true knowing or discrimination is the belief that everything is God's *maskrade* or *Isvara Lila* and living your life according to that belief. Being deluded by God's play is not a sin. It is only immaturity. I do not say do not sin. I say stop being a silly boy or girl but be a man or a woman.

How to remember God all the time?

I have said that remembering God all of the time and doing one's duties in the world should go together. I will illustrate this by an example. A man X had a friend Y whom he loved and respected. They did not meet for many years. Then news came to X that Y was dead and that his only son was an orphan, his mother having died earlier, and that he was in difficulty. Now X was the proprietor of a large organization, and he arranged for the boy Z to be brought to him and he gave Z an appointment in his organization, and arranged for his stay, food etc. X treated Z with love and wisdom because Z was the son of Y. Even if Z turned out to be a bad boy and was ungrateful to X, if X really loved Z because he was the son of Y, he would treat him with love and wisdom.

What I have written above is an explanation of how to remember God all of the time and also do your duty in the world. If you remember yourself as *Isvara Putra* and also see everyone else the same, you will never forget God as you live.

SADHANA C

Righteous Living With A Service Spirit to God: Subjective

Be a Devotee of God
Surrender to God
Be a Server of God
Serve God and Reknow Your Service as God's play
Accept All that Happens to You as Gifts from God
Meditate on God

God-meditation is the aim of all spiritual practices. It becomes capable of being maintained for some length of time, only if your life in the world is also lived for God. It means meditation cannot become possible without right-eous living with a service spirit to God. Being so the *sadhana*s to achieve it have been stated and explained.

Be a Devotee of God
Isvara bhakti

From Desire to Devotion

To me, devotion means devotion to God. Devotion is called *bhakti*. The great desideratum of spiritual life is to move away from worldly desires to devotion to God.

Devotion to God is the first result of accepting oneself as an offspring of God or *Isvara Putra*. The new life begins when one becomes mindful of the presence of God within oneself as the Player of one's life. This intimate relationship is always available to everyone, just as sunlight is available to all. God's communion within us is always available. It is you who have to become conscious of this fact and learn to open your heart more and more to God. An acceptor of this philosophy is immediately a lover of God and is destined for a non-dual Union or At-one-ment with God, because he or she is God's already. It is only a question of time.

Longing for At-one-ment with God

Devotion to God means an intense longing for the non-dual At-one-ment with God. It is the great goal of human life. It is a pure blissful experience and a state of Perfect Spiritual Health. Even a mere intense longing for God will lead you to that state. In worldly matters if you go on longing for a goal without doing what ought to be done to attain it, you will never attain it. But if you can long for the non-dual At-one-ment with God with all your heart, soul, and mind like a girl mad for the contact with her lover, even if you do not do anything about it, God will take you Himself. So the intensity of longing for the non-dual At-one-ment with God matters more than the spiritual practices. It is not that spiritual practice is not important but without an intense longing for the goal, it will be a dry practice and it will take time.

To put it differently, devotion to God is the longing to become God-like. What pleases God is that you should aspire after His likeness. Jesus said, "Be ye perfect, as your Lord is perfect." When you attain God's likeness you will have nothing to get and nothing to do but most people want as the fruit of devotion, that they should be able to get and do what they are now unable to get and do.

You should cultivate devotion to God. The cultivation of devotion to God is not wrong because what is sought to be accomplished through cultivation, is only an awakening of your true nature that spontaneously loves and feels at home with things pertaining to the Eternal. Willed devotion may not go with knowledge of your true identity, but true devotion does.

Love of God and Contemplation

Usually God has been defined associating Him with a form but it is possible to love God in the abstract. By love of God I mean all efforts to directly commune with Him without going through the world. Thus love of God equates with contemplation. God is pleased by our efforts to understand Him, and by our efforts to understand ourselves in relations to Him, and by our love for Him. Let me explain. There is a trust that owns some charitable institutions and it has sufficient funds at its disposal. A woman is appointed as the manager of the trust properties. She knows that the philanthropist who has established the trust lives in a foreign country. She knows his name but she knows nothing more about him. Being a conscientious woman, she imagines the gentleman and manages the trust in such a way that she believes that would please him. Similarly, you can imagine what would please God to the best of your ability and live your life according to it. You may say, "The woman has a concept of a man that is clear to her but with God there is no such basic concept and therefore it is hard" True, it is more difficult here, and the difference and the greater difficulty are granted. But still it would be possible for you to exercise your love for God through an abstract conception. If you reflect a little bit, you will understand that in the above example, physical attributes would play a very small part in the mind of the woman.

God is to be understood from His visible work, which is Creation. Just as from their physical activities we understand persons, from the government of a king we understand the king, so also from the happening of the phenomenal world we should understand God. No doubt this is difficult. But a determination to understand God in this way must be taken up.

Desire for the Eternal Realm

The nature of the mind is to go towards those matters which it desires or hopes to obtain happiness from. I have spoken of two realms of existence: the mundane that we now know, and the Eternal which we do not know but should know. Our desires are now towards the ephemeral, and desire when it is turned to the Eternal is called devotion. Devotion to God can be called the desire for the other realm of existence. Let me explain. Physically an individual is where his body is. Mentally, an individual is where his mind is. In both cases, the individual is where he wants to be. In truth, we are with God. We are sleeping in Heaven and dreaming this earthly life. Because now we are one with our minds, we feel estranged from God, and influenced by the world. To discover that we really are with God, the way has to be by making the mind go towards Eternal.

Devotion and Knowledge

Devotion to God and the knowledge of one's true identity should be understood as connected. The more the son, who has forgotten himself and knows himself, the more his natural love of his father will return. The beginning of devotion to God is knowledge of God. Without knowledge of God there can be no devotion to God. Even love at first sight requires sight. One cannot fall in love without meeting and knowing a person but one can meet and know a person without falling in love. When a mother notices her daughter behaving strangely and she diagnoses the symptoms as love, she wonders who the man is that her daughter has met, and loves. So love is the effect of knowledge and the evidence of it. Just as knowledge is the beginning of devotion, devotion is the end of knowledge.

The aim of the path of devotion and the path of knowledge are the same, which is that one must disown and disclaim the unreal, and become restored to the Real. In the path of devotion, all of our affections now directed towards worldly objects must be weaned away from them and directed towards God. To turn the flow of feeling from going towards objects of the world and to direct it towards God is the path of devotion or *bhakti yoga*. The path of knowledge or *gnana yoga* seeks to achieve the same end by a culture of the knowing faculty. The knower is taught to perceive the unreality of everything that is cognizable including the I-thought. By a very special and subtle teaching the disciple is taught by the guru to apprehend Reality which is not an object of outward knowing, but is *That* by which the knower derives his power of knowing.

How to Cultivate Devotion

Devotion begins with thinking of God. By thinking of God you will increase in your understanding and love of Him. How to think of Him? This is the question that intellectuals have to face.

My recommendation is this: think of God to start with as the sole controller of your life who is also the sole controller of all lives. You can infer God by directly thinking of Him as your Inner Ruler and Controller or *Antaryami* without bringing in the scriptures.

Breath controls you. He controls breath. Your body with its appetites and needs control you. He controls your body, and its appetites. Your mind and its nature control you. He controls your mind. The subconscious controls you. He controls your subconscious. Past tendencies control you, and He controls them. You live by knowing and understanding. He controls your cognitive faculties and functions. You live by feelings and emotions, and He controls your feelings and emotions. You have the experiences of pain and pleasure. He controls them. The environment holds you very much in its influence. He controls the environment. God is the controller of all the faculties of your living namely the instruments of action, the instruments of cognition, breathing, and mind, intellect, ego, and memory.

Let all activities, both inner and outer remind you of God who is the controller of them. Let your waking, dreaming, and sleeping states remind you of God who is the controller of them. Let the objects of your knowing remind you of God. Remembering God, which is cultivated by remembering the five truths, will lead to devotion and surrender to Him. It will lead to a service spirit and acceptance, and culminate in meditation. Empirically God's control is lawful. By verbal testimony we understand that His Grace is behind His government.

Love of God is fostered by the repeatedly uttering God's Name or *Nama japa*. You can address God by the name that is familiar to you but the name should mean the Player of your life and the Inner Ruler and Controller of your mind.

How should a devotee live in this world? Let me explain. A girl who lives in a place X meets a man who has come from a place Y. He goes away, saying that after one year he will come and take her away from X to Y and marry her. This man from Y has no connection with X. How would the girl live in X until the man from Y comes to take her? Most of her mind would be with the man of Y and her activities in X would become a bare minimum. In short, she would not engage in those activities that cannot relate to him and his pleasure and would only engage in such activities that will relate to him and his pleasure. Similarly, the world can be considered to be either a place unconnected with God or a theater fashioned by God for rightful living. In either case, the devotee will not engage in activities that are not meaningful in terms of God, and will only engage in those activities that are meaningful in terms of God. What are such meaningful acts? The devotee will become able to say, "Everything that I do is to serve God and thereby please Him. All that I experience in my life is incurred in His service. I live for Him in the consciousness of being with Him as I do so. In short, I am for Him, I feel for Him, I think for Him, I speak for Him, I act for Him."

Lose your self-consciousness in the thought of God. This is the final instruction or *upadesa*.

Surrender to God
Prapatti

Starting Point of Spiritual Life

In some respects, surrendering to God is the starting point of spiritual endeavor, and the principal of the spiritual endeavor, and all other spiritual endeavors are its limbs. Let me explain. After, understanding the five truths which tells you that your highest good is the non-dual At-one-ment with God, the first proper act that you should do is this. You should discard your previous life lived on the idea that you are a person, and discard your previous way of thinking that improving your person is your value. You should commit yourself wholly to the Lord to be guided, taught, and awakened by Him to realize your non-dual At-one-ment with Him.

Become Espoused to God

When a girl has understood which of the various men is fit and qualified to be her husband, she should leave all other loyalties and become espoused to him. If she does not do so, but respects him, learns from him, and serves him, she is not his wife. Surrender is, as it were, to become apprenticed to God, to become his wife. When I use the word wife, I have the following intentions. The husband and wife are of equal existence or *samasatta* and in their union they derive indescribable happiness, far more than the objects and persons of the world can give. You should understand that you are really a soul even now, and you, as a soul and God are same kind. Surrendering to God is like becoming affianced, and liberation is like nuptials.

Surrender Your Choice

Generally in surrendering, one expresses his or her consent to be completely governed by the will of another on all matters. Surrender is the complete acceptance of the sovereignty of another over oneself. The conquered in a battle may surrender in this way to the conqueror. When one is completely dominated by another without one's willingness, the non-surrendering attitude increases the pain of the captivity. When one is completely and helplessly under another's control, the acceptance of that fact reduces the pain but it cannot end it. When one loves the captor adequately, then the suffering can end, by surrendering.

But surrender to God is different from this. God has given us freedom and He wants us to use it rightly. He wants our cooperation. In worldly surrender, the captive is made to do things or told what to do; he is not asked to choose for the master. God, however, wants us to cooperate with Him in choosing for Him.

Choice and surrender can go together when a good son chooses but always accepts the dispensation of his father without demur. A loyal and devoted employee in an organization may also do this. So, as a conscious *Isvara Putra* you should choose for God in the living of your life. At the same time you should not forget that your goal is freedom of choice. You should aspire for that State where you will be freed from choice in the living of your life. The way to freedom of choice is through Pro-God life. You should approach it by aspiring for God's conduction or *prerana* in your life. Living for God will enable you to get God's Conduction. So, 'pray for God's Conduction' (*Prarthana* for *Prerana)* is the mantra I suggest in regard to the well-known spiritual practice that goes by the name of surrender.

You may ask, "How do I express my aspiration for God's conduction?" The answer is that it must be expressed in the way you live with your choice. Pro God Choice is the way of freedom from choice rather 'Pro God Choice with Right Awareness' is the way of freedom from choice.

Offer Your Entire Life to God

The highest kind of surrender is this. The physical body with its motor organs, sense organs, the mind, the cognizing, thinking, feeling, and experiencing faculty, and the environment of persons and objects are all made and fashioned by God. They have given to us for our use by God and He is administering them according to our manner of use of them. To be intelligently and fully conscious of this is to be conscious of our dependence on God. With an increasing consciousness of dependence, the sense of egoism decreases, and the feeling of 'I do' is replaced by the knowledge 'Enabled by Him I do'. This dependence, which goes with the offering of one's entire life to God, is the higher kind of surrender.

The Process of Surrender of Freedom

God does not determine our volition. We are free agents, but dependently free agents and not independent totally free agents. Thus although God has given us 'freedom of choice' and is only governing us in our use of it, nevertheless He is pleased when the freedom is surrendered to Him as it were. But it is not easy to surrender our freedom to God. If we can do so, instantaneously we will be liberated from all cares and responsibilities. So, the surrender of freedom has to be done gradually as the consummation of a process. What is that process?

First, one should sufficiently master the tendencies of self-seeking by doing spiritual practices. Then one should go by the spirit of righteousness or *dharma* and not by the letter of righteousness or *dharma*. This means that we do not do what we like but we do what we sincerely feel God would like us to do in such and such a situation. I call this Pro-God Thinking. One should train oneself to consult God first before doing anything. The next step is not so much to think Pro-God, as to listen inwardly and to wait for His guidance.

The last step is not so much to act, but to be a passive instrument or a medium for God's action taking place through us. Jesus said, "It is not I that do the work you see me do. It is God in me that does the work."

Be a Server of God
Isvara D<u>a</u>san

Living Depending on God

A server of God or an *Isvara d<u>a</u>san* or a *d<u>a</u>san* is the one who makes of his entire life an offering that is acceptable to God. A *da̱san* will live his or her life with the consciousness of depending on God for everything, and depending *only* on God for all his or her requirements. As I have said earlier, our physical bodies and our intellects and the environment of persons and objects are all made by God and they have been given to us for our use by God and He is administering them according to our manner of use of them. So, to be intelligently and fully conscious of this is to be conscious of our dependence on God. With an increasing consciousness of dependence, the sense of egoism decreases.

Living Unselfishly

A dependent devotee or a *da̱san* can be selfish or unselfish. Of course the dependent devotee will be a righteous devotee even if he or she is a selfish devotee. I call such people righteous selfish devotees. One can also be a righteously selfish without bringing in God. But a server of God, who is unselfish, is different from the righteous selfish devotee.

Viewing All Works as God's Work

A server of God or a *da̱san* should be conscious of always acting in the service of the King of kings because his or her body is God's mask or *Isvara Ve̱sham*. He must know that his body is a uniform of God reminding him that it belongs to God and that it must be employed in His service. Generally officers wear uniforms appropriate to the service that they are rendering. Policemen wear uniforms, as do generals, and soldiers. Judges too wear wigs when pronouncing judgements. An officer wears a uniform while he or she is on duty. But he can cast his uniform aside, when he is not on duty and relax. You, however, can never cast aside your uniform until liberation, which you are and should be alert in His duty, all the time. (The words 'you are' refer to you as a person). You should be always conscious of being on duty in His Divine Majesty's Service because your very physical body is your uniform being God's mask or *Isvara Vesham*. How can you relax?

A server of God should view all the works in the world as God's work. Let me explain. There was a fairly successful contractor, who received temple work contracts along with his other contracts. But this made no difference to him because he charged the same rate and did the same quality of work for both the temple works and ordinary jobs. One day he heard a spiritual storyteller and his mind changed. He began to do the temple works with great joy and dexterity. He used his own materials but charged only the cost price for them and he did not charge for his personal skill and supervision. Later he heard another modern preacher, say, Mr. R. V (Remaji is referring to himself) and his mind underwent yet another change. He began viewing all works as God's works and he did them with joy and earnestness and charged equally for temple works and ordinary works, and his efficiency and dexterity was the same in both cases.

Let the practitioners of this exposition proceed from the first to the second and then from the second to the third, or if they can, go directly to the third level from the first.

Cultivating A Loving Attitude and Right Thinking

A conscious server of God or a *dasan* should cultivate a democratically loving attitude towards the great variety of people who live - the rich and the poor, the good and the bad etc. This means that he or she should act in every situation in such a way that if others acted similarly in similar situations God's intention for all human beings would be advanced as far as he can see it. All his thoughts should spring from the basic attitude that he is an offspring of God or *Isvara Putra*, but ignorant of his true identity and deluded by God's play, or *maskrade*.

A conscious server of God or a *dasan* should think of everybody as an end in themselves. Therefore he or she should be judged not only by what he does, but also by how he thinks about others. Many social reformers and some such people fall into the error of regarding people as so many "fodder" for their good intentions and programs.

Serve God and Reknow your Service as God's play
Isvara Seva

Ascertain God's Will and Serve

The first duty of a server of God or a *dasan* is to become conscious of God, whose 'Will' he or she has to serve, as is always with him, right behind him, pressing on him. He should understand that he exists completely in Him, as does a child in its mother's womb. He should not forget that he is totally and completely involved in God's creative sport, and should become sensitive to God's creational embrace of his life. This will help him attune his will to God's. The anxiety to attune into 'God's 'Will' will immediately reduce his ego or pro-self will. *This is the meaning of embracing a life of righteousness*.

Now the question arises, does God have a Will for us? Yes. First, we should understand that this world has a Creator, who has His Will regarding every matter, and He wants us to experience that we are not different from Him. A real genuine love for God is that which expresses itself as in a tremendous concern and anxiety to know

God's Will, and to assist it by what one does, and not thwart it.

Generally, love for a person that does not express itself in a great concern to understand and further his or her will is not genuine. Only in the case of children or an immature person can love not do this because the will of the person may not be for his own good and it may do harm to the loved one to do his will in all situations. But such a problem does not exists with regard to wise people, real saints, and God. A server of God can unconditionally seek to ascertain and serve God's Will.

Serve With Love but Without Attachment

Most people are only capable of attachment or else they are indifferent. They make use of people for their own purposes, and when they are finished with their purpose they cast them off, or, they become attached to the persons. If people are neither useful nor are they such as one can be attached to them, then indifference follows. A server of God should be neither attached nor indifferent, but highly concerned and interested in others without attachment to them.

The liberated or the perfect sons of God will do their duty by kith and kin, unattached to them as if they were strangers, and they will care for strangers as if they are their kith and kin. But the good sons of God or *conscious Isvara Putras* should treat every one as belonging to God, because in truth every one is a son of God, an *Isvara Putra*, and they should aspires to become perfect sons of God. The future well being of the world *depends* on the good sons of God or *conscious Isvara Putras*.

Good sons of God should first correct their motive, and after establishing their motive well enough, then they should correct their sense of agency in their activities by understanding that the Lord is the real agent. Or know the qualities or *gunas* of MA, the Creative Power of God, as the agent.

Service to Humanity is the Proof of Devotion

Appreciation is the fruit of understanding and the proof of it. Love of the creature is the fruit of the understanding of the Creator and the proof of it. Love of God without love of mankind is suspect. I said earlier that love of God is the fruit of knowledge and the proof of it. In another manner of speaking, love of one's fellow man is the fruit of, and proof of, love of God. Subjectively, love of God is the fruit of knowledge, and objectively, the service to God is the proof of devotion. Love of man without love of God may not be stable. It may be tainted by defects of sentiment or selfishness. When a mankind is wisely loved, that love will include the understanding of God in it.

Why should a wise love of fellow man include an understanding of God? Are there not so many examples of beautiful and pure love without God coming in? We can discuss separately.

Conscious Living for God

We are all unconscious servers of God. By every action that we do we change our selves and we change the environment of objects and persons, both for the better and for the worse. India has awakened to the significance of the former. The *karma theory* states that for every action that a man does he makes himself liable to certain results in the future. But the fact that all our activities changes the environmental condition effects a change in the geographical, social and cultural environment has not been taken into account. This presentation of Higher Wisdom takes both into account, but makes the latter the central article of the new life that man is called upon to live.

We influence not only the physical environment by what we do which is obvious, but we also influence the choice of values by which men live. Let me explain. If a father eats carelessly, leaving food on his plate, his son is also influenced to eat carelessly, and the mother has a harder task to make the son eat properly. This is overt or physical influence. But what I want to say is, there is also a subtler covert influence. There is as it were a universal moral climate which influences everybody, and which is being fashioned by the nature of our choices. If this is accepted, our moral responsibility seems to be greater than we think. If a person fall, he makes it subtly easier for others to fall, and by rising, he subtly makes it easier for others to rise also. Please note, that here I am referring to a hidden covert influence and not to the overt influence by which the values of one affects those of others. Therefore we must get out of the habit of thinking about and acting and living for oneself, and get into the habit of thinking, acting, and living for God.

Your Service Too Is Contained In God's Play

A lover of God is a server of God and his life is a service to God. Servers of God will respond to God's Will and they will be the righteous co-players with Him in His play or *Masque* or *Lila*. They will know everything as God's, and they will think, speak, and do in the sprit of service to God. After performing their activities in the service of God they will offer their service to Him by reknowing them as a part of God's play. They know that their service too is contained in God's play as a part of it and not apart from it. They know that nothing they do, speak, think, feel, or experience are not apart from God's play, or *maskrade* or *Isvara Lila*, which is enacted through their free will. Therefore they will not attach themselves with their activities.

Accept all that Happens to You as Gifts from God
Samattva buddhi with Isvara prasada bhava

General Meaning of Acceptance

The general meaning of acceptance is to accept everything that happens to oneself without resisting it or desiring a change. Acceptance is the opposite of desiring a change. We all know however, that the world is always changing whether we desire a change or not; therefore we can say that acceptance is not resisting a change.

There are people who accept their lot in life and they do not desire a change in it. This is a simple position. There are those who are so placed in life that they have no freedom of choice. Women in old Hindu homes are like that. There was a round of duties that she had to perform. The woman would keep on performing them and accept all that happens.

There are also partial acceptances. A man after fifty may accept that women in the world are no longer interested in him romantically. An employee may become resigned to a state of no more promotions. All of us are acceptors in certain matters.

Understanding God's Intention for Us Makes Acceptance Easy

A woman undergoing a beauty treatment from an expert will submit to any amount of physical torture to have her beauty augmented. When the reward is known to her to be what she very much wants, she will put up with the dispenser's dispensations what ever they maybe.

The beauty specialist need not like the woman, for her to endure his tortures. But if she also knows his love for her, her enduring will be all the easier. So also, what God wants to give us is so very great, that if we only understand it, we will not at all mind the troubles we have to undergo en route to it. Of course, God's love for us is shown to us by His wanting to give us His Kingdom. But still you must want it.

Various Ways of Acceptance

Acceptance can come in the following ways. It can come from sheer experience, from a sense of "Life is like that, it has its ups and its downs. We must take things as they come." It can come from the understanding "All things are happening according to my actions or *karma*. In every event certain change takes place and it expends itself. By my accepting it, I can refrain from adding to it. Therefore, let me accept all the good and bad, and keep on moving, and live and work in a spirit of acceptance." Acceptance can also come from the understanding that all is the gift of God or *Isvara prasadam*, and we can pleasure Him by accepting His dispensations without protesting as they come. This is a variety of the second.

Accepting what happens as a gift of God is acceptance. You should learn to accept all happenings as gift from God. They are acceptable because the giver is more important that the gift. Accepting the results of all happenings as God's gift according to one's action or *karma*, and acting in every situation Pro-God will decrease the estrangement from Him and increase the non-dual At-one-ment with Him.

Acceptance is broadly of two kinds: acceptance of events as and when they occur, and acceptance of one's entire life condition whatever it may be at every moment.

Acceptance Improves Mental Health

Acceptance of all happenings is the desideratum. Acceptance is neither protest nor acquiescence. Acceptance is not resignation or complacency. It should be understood that action to change a situation could arise only from acceptance, whereas it does not arise from resignation. Acceptance is not tolerance. To accept things without a sense of resignation or defeat is an important virtue.

Acceptance is a form of forgiving. Through acceptance, the experiences of both the joy and the sorrows of the memory will be removed, and the wisdom of the memory will then be free to operate. Acceptance is best practiced regarding the events of one's past life, and its proper consummation will make a tremendous difference to one's mental health.

Acceptance is Equanimity of Mind

In one way acceptance of a situations is equanimity of mind. Equanimity is established, when the failures and successes of the past become equally meaningless, when the terms friend and enemy do not mean what they once meant, and being loved and not being loved are matters of personal indifference. It is established when nothing is desired and when nothing about the future is feared. Equanimity does not mean that one should equate good and bad music, or poverty and affluence. Good music is not bad music, and poverty is not affluence. What is meant is that both have no charm or the opposite for the established spiritual practitioner. It means that he has no interest, so he does not judge.

Because he has no value to achieve in the mundane, he does not bother to judge anything. He is a man of equanimity of mind only in that sense. In a way it is like the attitude of a child to the values of the world.

Acceptance Makes You a Choiceless Admirer of God's Art

A server of God should remember that God's artistic perfection is great in a wholly bigger dimension. He should learn to look at the play of God or *rass God's maskrade* from that dimension. If he does so, he will become a choiceless admirer of God's play of his life in all vicissitudes. Let me explain.

There was a religious ceremony at Mr. Kumar's house. Many close relatives and friends attended the function. At the end of ceremony Mrs. Kumar ordered her daughter to sing a song to conclude the function. The daughter was conscious of her mediocre talent and does not want to sing but her mother insisted. With a heavy heart and unwillingness to perform, the girl hesitantly walked into the middle of the gathering and sang with a defeated mentality. It was a terrible performance. At the end, with tears in her eyes the girl left the room. A member of the audience, who happened to be an actress, followed the girl and said, "Tomorrow I have to act in a scene exactly what happened here to you right now. I worried about how I was going to do it. You have shown me how to act in that situation, like a great director would show me. I come here to pay my respects to you."

You should Accept God's Government

You should accept, all happenings because, they are permitted by God in His design and government of the universe. Life presents both good and bad. No doubt a considerable part of life's evil is remediable and removable. But a considerable part will remain as a part of the design of life. For example, we live with a body, (which *must* be at its best in youth and then decline and die) that has beautiful pure eyes, and dirty organs of evacuation. We live in the world that has spring-season, and the hot and wet cold seasons. The trees are sometimes in full bloom, and at other times they are barren. We must learn that the design of life itself includes both good and bad and clean and dirty, and we must learn to take the good with the bad in the proper way, neither with total resignation, nor with a seething protest but with a dynamic acceptance.

The more that a person accepts with understanding that God's Will governs all things, the better things will be for him. Mental discontent, aggrieved, and resentment are all signs of the non-acceptance of divine dispensations with regard to the circumstances and happenings of your life. "Everything is happening according to the government of God." is what the understanding of great souls.

But acceptance need not require theism behind it. Suffering is due to the non-acceptance of facts and this should be realized clearly. How can good thinking and good action result from the non-acceptance of facts? First, facts must be accepted and rightly understood. Then the unreality of the facts should be sought, and to be understood. Acceptance of God's government as His Grace in disguise reduces pain and hastens the process of our liberation.

Devotion and Knowledge Help Acceptance

There are two ways to become acceptors. One is through devotion and the other is through knowledge. They may coalesce also. How can devotion to God help acceptance? This should be gone into thoroughly. But a simple answer that I have already given is that a gift from one who is loved will be accepted whatever the nature of the gift. Every thing that befalls us happens under God's dispensation, and thus he who loves the dispenser should accept His dispensation. When a lover invites you to his house, and he is next to you with his arms around you, can you be discontent with the furniture and comforts in the room? So, whether you are rich or poor in your living conditions, God is with you. Learn to rejoice in this truth, and let His being with you be sufficient wealth for you. And out of the joy of the thankfulness of His being with you, act in ways that express that joy and do not act to make a living. This is one argument.

How can knowledge help acceptance? All experiences take place in the play of God, and therefore they are not really real. The sufferer, the cause of suffering, and the experience of suffering all belong to the Play of God. Our real being is above/trance God's play. Thus the intelligent contemplation of, 'I am That and all this is not really real' is in brief the way to attain the attitude of acceptance, using by knowledge.

Acceptance and Desireless Action

Let me consider acceptance and the path of desireless action or *Karma yoga*. Life consists in the main of reactions to actions. In a boxing match, each fighter both inflicts blows and suffers blows. When he inflicts a blow, he acts and when he suffers a blow, he reacts. Reaction and action continually follow one after the other in our lives. These can also be called impression and expression.

The point to understand is this. In one level of speaking, reaction is in our control but action is not so much in our control. For example, if someone insults you, you are fully in charge of controlling your reaction to his insult. But giving him back in his own coin may be or may not be possible for you.

So, equanimity is making a worship of our reactions to circumstances and desireless actions or *Karma Yoga* is making a worship of our actions in the world. In another word acceptance is the worship of God in reaction. Action with a disinterested attitude in the results is the worship of God in action.

Acceptance from Higher Level of Understanding

Acceptance of happenings as God's gift comes from faith. There is a higher acceptance, however, that comes from *understanding the laws of God's government.* What ordinary people call miracles takes place according to the higher laws of God's government. Cooperation is spontaneous and effortless when one understands God's government fully. No one has done it so far except perhaps Buddha.

Acceptance will enable us to attain the highest level of consciousness, to transcend the level of duality. In a way, acceptance in its full and proper meaning, is a kind of liberation.

Meditate on God
Isvara Dhyanam

God Meditation

Generally, meditation is a thoughtless, dynamic attention upon an object, mental or material. Thoughtless attention is not be possible unless desire (at least for the time being) regarding the object is laid aside. You should be clear about this.

The way to know God as your real identity is God meditation. God meditation is the attempt to deepen your consciousness, more and more until soul or *Isvara Putra* consciousness is attained. The object of God meditation is the knowledge of God. The culmination of God meditation is that the meditater becoming the object of meditation. Now, one cannot become another unless one is already the other, and only ignorance and delusion stand in the way of experiencing it. The scriptures declare that such is the case, and that God is our real identity. By God meditation we can free ourselves from ignorance and delusion, and experience God as our real identity. When we experience our non-dual At-one-ment with God, we will also experience the world as being inside us.

Sincere Longing for God is God Meditation

Longing for the experience of God or *Antaryami darsan*, who is ever with you in the depths of your own being, is God meditation. In a way, meditation i s performed by all of us on the worldly matters which we long for, hope for, and crave. If these cravings are many, the dynamic energy is scattered, and the cherished objects are not realized. If one longs for only one object with all of his mind, intellect, and heart, the conditions are the most favorable for his getting it. Similarly, sincere longing for the non-dual At-one-ment with God with all your heart and mind is the starting point of God meditation. An intelligent and earnest pondering on the five truths will bring this into effect.

God Meditation Purifies the Mind

God meditation is like the cleansing of a mirror by someone who is standing before it. Here cleansing the mirror is not only making the glass clean but also making its surface pure. When the mind is pure and clean, the reflection represents the original without distortion. When this is done, the cleansing work ceases. The problem has vanished by burning away mental impurities. Burning away the mind itself as it has functioned in the past promote the non-dual At-one-ment with God.

The matter can be understood in another way also. The soul was blind, and was unable to see God, or its own self, or the hosts of angels in heaven. It was given the mind to see only this world of God's *maskrade* or *Maya Lila*. It is like a man without independent sight, wearing spectacles, by which to see. The wearer is asked to use the sight through the spectacles, not to merely enjoy sights, but to correct the vision. When the vision is perfectly corrected, the spectacles fall off. Likewise God has conjoined us with the mind to awake us from our primordial ignorance. Therefore we must use our mind not merely to 'enjoy and succeed' in the world, but to make the mind pure. When the mind is purified, it beholds the world as God's divine play upon which the mind and the play disappear in the vision of Heaven or vision of Eternal Home or *Darsan of Nithyavibhuti*.

The modus of how God meditation purifies the mind can also be understood through the concept of delusion or *moha*. I will put it like this. Both in bondage before liberation and in liberation after bondage, the three factors, namely God, soul and the mind or *Rader*, *Isvara Putra* and *maskrader*, will be present. What then will be absent in one case but present in the other case to distinguish between bondage and liberation? The answer is delusion. Delusion will be present in bondage and will be absent on liberation. Suffering will be present in bondage and will be absent on liberation.

Meditate on the Five Truths

The way to end ignorance and achieve non-dual At-one-ment with God Consciousness is through an intense contemplation of God. But this contemplation will be difficult unless your misknowing of God's play as your life is sufficiently reduced. I recommend the five sacred words of the five truths that I have discussed in the way of life for meditation. When they get established, your misknowing of God's play will be replaced by the true knowing, and thoughtless consciousness will come to be. What will remove your suffering is the meaning of the sacred word or *mantra* and not the sound of the *mantra*. But first train your mind with the repetition of the *mantra*, and then assimilate the meaning of the *mantra*. The higher stage is when you can get the meaning of the *mantra* without the help of the utterance of the *mantra*.

In your present condition of defective cognition you must think of both God and the Foundation or in other words *R_ader* and RA as being behind your knowing consciousness, and your ego and thoughts or in other words the *maskrader* and *maskrades* being in front of you. Contemplate God as your Sustainer, and the RA as your Foundation. Liberation lies in becoming more and more conscious of your Sustainer and the Foundation. For that you must consciously remember that you are an *Isvara Putra*, deludedly identifying with your life, and remember God as the undeluded Witness of your life. I have already told you that there is no harm in identification, but the 'delusion' in identification is the problem. So, understand firmly that your *hope* lies *only* on becoming more and more a Witness, like God, your Eternal Father. God is the Lord of the world, and the Knower of His Substratum Self. So God is in a position to bestow on you, the good thing of this world, and also the supreme good. If, this understanding maintained, the undivided attention in the contemplation of God would be facilitated. The first fruit of meditation can be considered to be the achievement of a contemplation of God with uninterrupted and undivided attention.

I suggest the following to the good sons and daughters of God. You should meditate on the five truths at times, remember the truths all the time, and serve others many times until the practice gets natural to you. Also as the first act of every morning on getting up you should pray like this: Oh Inner Ruler and Controller protect me. To know my being as not different from You, and to know my life as Your play, shall be the goal of my life, and to realize this truth in my immediate direct experience, I shall hence forward direct the energies of my living.

Contemplate God as the Witness of your Activities

According to my philosophy God is both the Player and the Witness or *Kridi* and *Sakshi*. Here I discuss the aspect of Witness.

God is the Witness of your inner life and your outer life. As you increase in the consciousness of God being Witness of all that is known, you will automatically increase in God Consciousness, that is the State of Witness of your inner and outer life. The known is conquered by the knowledge of Witness so contemplate God as Witness of your thoughts and actions.

A Brief Note on the State of Witness: Sakshi

Consciousness freed from identification with the instrument of perception and experience, is the State of Witness. The State of Witness can never be other than, Perfect and perfectly happy. The Witness being Perfect, cannot be improved. I say, you the soul or *Isvara Putra* are in truth a Witness. Now you may wonder like this, "If I am in truth a Witness, and Witness being Perfect, and cannot be improved, then who wants to become better?" The answer can be given in two ways. The ego wants to become better. Or you, a soul, an *Isvara Putra,* think that you are a person, and want to become better as a person. You, as person can improve, but can never become perfect and perfectly happy.

God has made you a subject and is making you dash against the objects of the world, and thereby evolving your consciousness. God has made you a knower. Knowers are either liberated or bound but Consciousness is always liberated. Bondage is unknown to it. Your true identity is Consciousness but now you are a deluded knower. Deluded knowers are called conscious beings or *chetanan*. The Witness is called Consciousness or *Chaitanya*. Take your choice what you shall be.

Let me take you one step further. Strictly speaking your true identity is not even a Witness. RA is your true Self and it is Infinite Awareness. The state of objectless awareness is your real Self or *Swarupa*. But I do not wish to distinguish the Player and the Absolute and make the Player less than Absolute because the Player *Knows* His Absolute Self. God is the Knower of the Self. God Knows His true Self as the Unchanging Awareness and also plays as the World. So, you, the offspring of God or *Isvara Putra*, by remembering the Player with love and serving Him by all that you do, will increase in the attributes of the Player. I would recommend that of all of the attributes of the Player, you should aspire most to increase in His State of Witness.

The Father is right behind you always with this intention. Firstly to develop you through deluded attachment to your person and ultimately to make you a Witness as He is. He wants your cooperation to do this job quickly. You must not forget this. The Father's Witnessing Consciousness must manifest in you. Witness is your birthright. When you become a Witness, you will also become the Witness of your ego and your life. When you become a Witness, problems will not disappear. As long as the world exists, problems will exist. But the ideas "my problem and my duty" will vanish and along with it your suffering will also vanish forever.

Almost all of you are strangers to the Bliss of Witness. You all want excitement by taking sides. But I say become a Witness. Increase in the awareness of Witness. You will become wiser. The partisans only become cleverer. Becoming Witness may take time. But let the intense desire to become a Witness awake and abide in you. Only He who knows Reality can be a Witness of the unreal. In the endeavor to be a Witness of the unreal, you will know the Real. The *Masque* or World or *Lila* is unreal and *R̲ader* or God or *Isvara* is Real. All these ideas will become clearer and clearer as time passes.

Right Expectation

To meditate on God for the betterment of your worldly life is considered to be inferior to the meditation upon Him for the non-dual At-one-ment with Him and becoming indifferent to the world. If you are capable of doing this, well and good. If you are not, however, then it will be good for you to meditate upon God for the non-dual At-one-ment with Him, and also for the betterment of your life. You should have the expectation that if you are able to do this well enough, you need take no thought about your life here, or your salvation in the here after. Until that stage is reached, you should feel obligated and take thought and live your life, to serve and please God.

Obstacles and Remedies of Meditation

A very rich couple had no child and prayed to God. God appeared before them and said, "A son will be born to you. But he will tell lies mostly. If you force him to tell the truth he will become weak. If you still force him to tell the truth he will run away and leave you." Our minds are like this boy. Our minds do not want to know the Truth. If you force it, it will become weak. If you further force it, it will reveal the Truth and disappear. That is why meditation is difficult. The mind does not like to be engaged in the inquiry of the Truth and meditation. So, first you should understand what is conducive and what is not conducive to meditation, and try to cultivate the former and remove the latter.

Some of the obstacles to and remedies for meditation are given below.

Obstacles

Non devotion to God, and not surrendering to God
Self-seeking and self-acting regarding one's body
    and one's life
Lovelessness regarding others, desire and hatred
Personal attachment and selfishness in thought
Unrighteous activities in thought, word, and deed
Mental perturbations in favorable and unfavorable
    Conditions

Remedies

Devotion to God, always remembering God, and
    surrendering to God
Discrimination of self and non self
Right knowing regarding others
Love and compassion regarding others
Pro God living
Acceptance of all that befalls one as blessings of God

Aspire for God-like Knowing and God-like Being
Practice knowing all as God's play
Practice doing all in His service

SADHANA D

Righteous Living With A Service Spirit to God: Objective

The following are the practices of sadhana D, which one should practice towards others. All the teachings that had been taught so far will help you to enrich your understanding of others and facilitate this practice.

Love others as you love yourself

Treat others in righteousness or *dharma*, and serve them as best as you can

Do not mind their adverse attitudes and activities

Enlighten them regarding their true identity and motivate them to cooperate with God for its realization when the circumstances are favorable

A Word of Caution

Sadhana D asks you to love others, to be of service to others, never to be offended by what they do and to be careful not to offend them. When you endeavor to treat others with love and wisdom for God's sake, some of the offspring of God may be ungrateful and unappreciative and even talk about you jeeringly. At that time you should heighten your spiritual practice with greater effort and continue your loving and wise treatment of them. Let me explain.

A wise and loving head of a household has living with him many sons, daughters, nieces, nephews, and in laws. Each is different - some are good and some are bad, some are cleaver and some are stupid, some are loyal and some are deceiving. But although the head loves them all, *basically* equally, his treatment of them would differ, because while love should rule in the heart, wisdom must govern the actual treatment of them. If you do not do this, and you make love-treatment *sentimentalism*, you will bring discredit to the very conception and ideal of love of others.

Love and Non-Differential Attitude

Love does not mean effusive sentimental gushing but rather non-differential attitude or *ananya buddhi*. Real love and a non-differential attitude go together. The understanding that all are offspring of God or *Isvara Putra*s gives the logical basis for non-differential treatment. Problems will not disappear by a non-differential attitude but one's attitude changes for the better.

Usually you react differently to a problem caused by X, who belongs to you or your group and the same problem caused by Y who does not belong to you. *Sadhana* D asks you to deal with problems caused by others with a non-differential attitude. When you have a non-differential attitude you treat others with the same consideration that you apply to yourself. It means that you do not use others as a means, but you relate with them as cooperators or *Isvara Putra*s in the realization that God has for all of His offspring.

You should learn not to be hurt. You should never be offended by what others do, and be careful not to offend them. Understanding the truth that every activity is God's play will make you suffer less by the bad behavior of people to you. The understanding that every person in truth an offspring of God, forgetful of their true identity and living a deluded life will make you forgive their faults. The world should not exist for you except to love, serve, and enlighten others. You should share this teaching with others when they are receptive. Let me explain.

In a mental hospital, a good doctor D is attacked, insulted, blamed, and criticized by the inmates who are mad in various ways and degrees. D is not indifferent to their behavior. How can he afford to be when he has the responsibility of curing them? But he is not offended by their behavior. Similarly the good offspring of God or conscious *Isvara Putras*, should not be offended by the misbehavior of others. Then only they can understand the true reason for their misbehavior, and take the proper steps for improvement. To correct others is an important thing. But before doing that, you should correct your own mind. I don't mean "Reform yourself before trying to reform others." That is different. I say, "Learn not to be hurt by the misbehavior of others, first." *Sadhanas* A and B will help here. A mind, which is hurt by the misbehavior of others, is spiritually ill. That mind is not a purified mind. It does not mean that you should not get angry by the misbehaviors of others. Many people do not get angry when others misbehave but they may be harboring resentments. Many people cannot afford to get angry. So not getting angry, and not being hurt are entirely different things. When you are hurtable, it means, that your mind is not sufficiently deepened. The deeper the understanding, the greater the forgiveness. Love is the greatest solvent of all ills. Love is unfathomably deep. So go on deepening, broadening, and widening your consciousness, until the entire of known is contained in it. Do not be contained in a part of the known, and confront the rest of the known. Let the entire known be contained in you.

Resentment Impedes Understanding

A clear understanding of the truth will relieve you of resentment. Let me explain. A king went hunting for a few days, and when he returned, he found a Monkey in his room. He got angry and drove it out with a stick. A few minutes later the queen came to him weeping, and she said that a yogi had come and that the king's son had insulted him. The yogi became very angry and cursed the boy to become a monkey. The queen said "I begged the yogi for forgiveness" and he said, "After ten days, he will be alright." How will the king treat his son now? He need not understand the monkey's mind and behavior. The knowledge "My son is temporarily in this condition" is enough. So the clear understanding that all are offspring of God or *Isvara Putra*s but do not know that they are due to their ignorance of their true identity and delusion towards their persons, is enough to make you accept their behavior without resentment. But you should not be content with acceptance. Understanding and efforts to improve them should follow. When they are willing to understand the truth, tell them that they are really offspring of God or *Isvara Putra*s but due to beginning-less ignorance they do not experience the truth. Explain to them that they are now living a deluded life and help them to understand that the removal of delusion and the experience of their true identity is their highest good.

GOAL OF LIFE

Direct Experience of the Five Truths:
Subjective and Objective

The supreme goal of life is the direct experience of the five truths, both subjective and objective. The way to attain it has been told in the 'way of life' in the form of four spiritual practices. After realizing the Truth in your own direct experience, it is not necessary for the verbal utterances of the truth. Only while talking to others, will you use those words.

Liberation requires a deep and long contemplation of the five truths. They are all tremendous truth, which requires years of discrimination and contemplation. Though the attainment of the supreme goal is far off, yet God's Conduction of one's life will increase with the intensity of *sadhana,* the spiritual practice and will be attended with benefits. You will experience an ultra mundane inner happiness unrelated to the outer circumstances of your life, and therefore not changeable by their change and not loseable by their loss. Your mental suffering will diminish. Your being will be completely and naturally undisturbed by the displeasing behavior of others, and your love and goodwill for them will continue undiminished. You will be able to say, "To me there is no such thing as displeasing behavior. There are misbehaviors. But I am not disturbed by the misbehavior of others. I try to understand the reasons for their misbehavior and do what I can, when I can, for their improvement." Your potential for good living will become enhanced. Also, due to increased God's Conduction in the activities of your life, the dexterity in your activities too will increase. You will feel better and fare better in the living of your life.

The supreme goal of life is achieved when the defective cognition evanesces completely. When that is done, you will experience in full, the Bliss of your non-dual At-one-ment with God. You will attain true knowing of what you know. By true knowing I mean that you will know your body, your ego and your life as *God's mask, maskrader* and *maskrade* or in other words as *Isvara Vesham, Isvara Nataka Patram*, and *Isvara Lila*. You will attain the State of Witness or *Sakshi* to the play of God. You will be an uninvolved spectator of God's play or *Isvara Lila* enacted in your passive Witnessing Consciousness. You will not have to act at all. You will be completely freed from suffering and you will find that the environment is not resisting your wishes.

In short, God-like Knowing and God-like Being are the supreme goal of life and fruits of your spiritual practice. After the death of the body, you will not be reborn again. The purpose of your embodied life in God's play is accomplished.

APPENDICES

Concept of Suffering and Artistic Delight

VEDANA AND RASANA

Your fundamental malady or the root cause of your suffering is due to defective cognition. To reknow your life as God's play and to cultivate an artistic gaze on it is the remedy for your malady. The right awareness of your ego, your body and your life as God's *maskrader*, mask, and *maskrade* will help you to cultivate an artistic gaze, and experience an artistic delight of your life. I call the artistic delight as *Rasana* and the suffering as *Vedana*. *Rasana* is a complete spiritual practice for the removal of ignorance and deluded attachment. Nothing in the world can equal the benefit of this spiritual practice. If you do so, you will experience your true identity, whose nature is Witness. Therefore let me explain the concept of suffering and the concept of artistic delight.

Suffering/*Vedana*

Vedana means suffering. Before I define what suffering is, let us understand the meaning of happiness. Regarding the meaning of happiness, one must distinguish between the common sense definition and the philosophical definition. Both have their purposes.

At a common level, happiness is that state of mind which, one is willing should continue, and unhappiness then would be that state of mind which one is not willing should continue. At a philosophical level, happiness is the absence of suffering and all (worldly) experiences is suffering. Therefore, philosophically, suffering means both pain and pleasure. In short all egocentric perturbations are suffering. Let me explain. When defeat overtakes us, we are depressed. That is suffering. When things are going well for us, we feel confident, optimistic, and in good spirit. That is also suffering. If a mother rocks her child and happily watches its calm face, in so far as there is a personal element in that experience, it is suffering.

Suffering in a mental condition is due to one's attachment to one's body and one's life. This attachment is so ingrained in us that many cannot even understand this statement. In short, suffering is due to the mis-knowing of persons and matters including oneself and therefore, mis-claiming them.

My philosophy does not propose an erasure of these two sufferings: pain and pleasure (which cause memo-ries). But it does propose a change in one's knowledge pertaining to these two classes of suffering. I call this *rasanic experience*. *Rasanic* experience belongs to the higher mind, which is undeluded. This philosophy asks you to look at the world and one's life in it as God's *maskrade* or *Isvara Lila*. By this new view of life, the suffering or *vedana* will be transmuted to artistic joy or *rasana*.

Artistic Joy/*Rasana*

A thing can be appreciated or *rassed* for its own sake. For example, a flower seller, when she enjoys the loveliness of her flowers apart from their usefulness to her to help her earn money, is *rassing* the flower. This can be called appreciation of beauty for its own sake. A thing can also be appreciated or *rassed* as the art of the person who produced it. For example, I hear a nightingale's sound. I listen with liking but there is no appreciation of the art of the producer in it. Then my friend says, "That sound is made by my neighbor." Now I appreciate or *rass* the sound in terms of an artist.

One can appreciate the art of a maker in the appearance of his artistic work. For example, a visitor upon entering a friend's house saw a cluster of bananas on a side table. They looked appetizing and the visitor was tired and hungry. He was considering whether he could waive the formalities and ask for some bananas to eat when the host, who had been reading his hungry gaze, interposed saying, "Those are not real bananas. They are made of wood." The visitor's desire disappeared and was replaced by an appreciation of the art of the maker in the appearance of the fruit. There is another type of appreciation of art. This is the appreciation of a beholder with regard to the play or acting of another. I call this artistic joy or *rasana*.

The concepts of *rasana* and *vedana* are correctly illustrated by dramatic awareness. Suppose that a rattling gypsy comes and begins crying and begging in front of your house. You think that this is a real beggar and you think how you will get rid of him. This attitude is suffering or *vedana*. When I notice your suffering I say, "That is not a real beggar. That is our fun loving friend Ram who has come to play a joke on us." Now your vision changes. You watch the gypsy with a new awareness and a new interest. I call the former *vedana* or a *vedanic* attitude and the latter *rasana* or a *rasanic attitude. Rasanic* knowing is to know the known not as an independent entity or as a thing or movement in itself, but is to know the known as the art-play or played art of an overt artist. It is the bliss of beholding the art of an artist (other than oneself). The artist I am referring here is God Himself.

The activity of the world is the art of God, the greatest of all artists. The world is God's artistic expression. It is God's Impersonational play. So, when one notices the world as God's artistic expression, one experiences the joy of *rasana* or the bliss of artistic delight.

Rasana is not wishing or liking. It is a double state of mind and ordinary people may confuse it with relishing or liking. *Rasana* is not to like suffering, whether it is pain or pleasure. That cannot be done and one will only sink into despair. The joy of *rasana,* is not carnal nor it is ego-centric satisfaction; it is the joy of aesthetic pleasure. It can be considered the reflection of bliss in life. Rasana should not be construed as supplanting the need for correction, but rather as furnishing the right basic attitude in which corrections should be attempted. This means that teachers should reprimand their students in a rasanic frame of mind, policemen should arrest the criminals with rasana, and masters should correct the inefficiencies and unrighteous behaviors of their servants with an attitude of *rasana*.

The true artist is more gratified by the artistic outlook of his art than by material rewards. So too, God the greatest of artists is pleased by our artistic outlook of His play, and rewards us with the bliss of *rasana*.

Whatever you see, you try to see it as artistic play of God. Whatever you see, you try to understand the truth of it, and understand it better. Whatever you see, you try to improve it, and beautify its condition. By all these you will please God immensely.

God Says to You

Do not see an enemy as a real enemy. See him or her as My *maskrader* and *maskrade*. See him or her as a challenge I am posing to you and think and act from that new understanding, and see what happens.

Brief Summary of the Four Spiritual Practices:
Sadhanas A, B, C, and D

You are a heavenly being living an earthly, mortal life. Your ignorance regarding your true identity and the subsequent delusion regarding your life is the fundamental cause of all of your problems or sufferings. The way to end your delusion and ignorance is to correct your defective cognition. When your knowing is corrected, thinking and doing will also be corrected.

Sadhanas A and B are the correctives for your defective cognition. They are the practice of the right awareness of the five truths, subjective and objective. The essence of *sadhana* A is to be conscious of the truths about God, you and your life. It is to be conscious of God as your Eternal Father, who is evolving you to attain His likeness and become a Witness like Him, yourself as His son or *Isvara Putra* and your life as God's play. Your life consists of your ego, your body and your activities. Therefore, to be aware of your ego, your body, and your life as God's *maskrader*, *mask*, and *maskrade* is to be conscious of your life.

To be more and more conscious of your life as God's play and to remember God as its Witness, and you belong to the Witness and not to the play is the backbone of this *sadhana*. This remembrance will make you objectify what you are not and will make you aspire and endeavor to become like God, a Witness. *Sadhana* B is to practice the same with regard to others. If you do so, it will reduce your discontent with yourself and all vexations with others. The right awareness of men and matters if practiced properly should reduce your delusions and attachments regarding them. If it does not, it means you are not practicing it properly.

Sadhanas C and D are the correctives for thinking and doing. They are the practice of righteous living with a service sprit to God, subjective and objective. The essence of these two practices is to love God and serve His world, which is to serve your fellow men or humanity on His behalf. The sincere practice of the four sadhanas will facilitate your meditation, which in turn will lead you towards your non-dual At-one-ment with God.

Remembering the truth is your primary duty. Though it is hard, it is not that hard. Are we not conscious of the days of the week effortlessly? The knowledge that today is Tuesday, or whatever it is, is always there, underlying all that we do, speak, and think. Is it not? Similarly you must remember the five truths, subjective and objective effortlessly all the time while living your life: speaking, doing and thinking. Your 'willed effort' is essential until you remember them effortlessly. Then they will become natural to you while living your life.

A Word on Willed Effort

The nature of donkeys is to amble slowly, and the nature of horses is to delight in running fast. A horse, forgetting that it is a horse, deludedly thinking that it is a donkey, is given to ambling slowly. Another horse asks this horse, "Why are you being a horse, ambling like a donkey?" The horse thus questioned replies "I am not a horse. I am a donkey and therefore I am ambling slowly." The other horse continues, "You are not a donkey. You have forgotten that you are a horse, and are deludedly thinking that you are a donkey. You are subject to both the ignorance of your 'horse-self' and the 'I am a donkey' delusion. I advise you to repeatedly say to yourself 'I am a horse' and practice running fast, by willed effort." The horse thus advised, did as advised, and in due course regained its 'I am a horse' knowledge, and thereafter delighted in running fast, naturally, and it stopped its ambling. If the animal in question was really a donkey, and not a horse, then the practice of saying repeatedly 'I am horse' and trying to run fast, would have only resulted in its becoming mad and breaking its legs. So too, you a conscious being, being really a son of God or an *Isvara Putra*, and not the body, by the practice of the four spiritual practices will regain the knowledge of your (ever attained) true identity.

God has given you choices in the living of your life. The main choice is this. You can live to be happy and successful according to your present conception, or you can live to attain a God-like State in the living of your life. To attain God-like State you must simply give up living for yourself and choose to live for God or Pro-God. By so doing you shall discharge your obligations to life better, and attain the main object of life.

Make your life a playful dialogue with God, the Great Player. He has bound you with good intent, He wants you to be free, and *He invites you to play the game with Him for becoming free*. In old stories, a knight has to perform deeds of valor to marry a chosen girl. Here God says, "Solve the problem that I have set you, and win Me and My Kingdom." I give a new spirit or a new *bhava* in which to seek and attain His Kingdom, the Eternal Abode.

What is it to live Religiously?

God is the Maker and the Maintainer of the body that you are using. The potter does not die when the pot is broken. The Maker of the body does not grow old and get sick when the body becomes old and sick, and die when the body dies. The Maker is Ageless, Immortal, Perfect, and Blissful.

You as an *Isvara Putra* are the user of the body. You also do not become old, sick and die when your body becomes old, sick and die. You are also immortal and perfect as the Maker is. It is not easy for the skeptical mind to accept the concept of the user of the body, but its acceptance is the beginning of religious life according to my teachings.

The difference between the Maker and user is that the Maker knows that He is immortal and perfect and altogether different from the mortal and imperfect bodies that He is making and maintaining. But the user does not know this. This is the one difference of the greatest significance and *the abolition of this difference is the supreme object of human life*. The religious life starts by accepting the above and aspiring to abolish the difference. Those who do so are, *reborn or dvijas.*

Users are the sons, disciples, and servants of the Maker. The Maker is the Player of the world and also the Witness of it. The Maker is God.

The play of God is performed for the enlightenment of the offspring of God, the embodied souls. *For the embodied souls to understand this and Consciously Cooperate with God is to live religiously.*

The to be worshipped is the Maker of the body
The worshipper is the user of the body
The instrument of worship is the body
The worship consists in the right use of or living with the body
The reward of worship is the bliss of the non-dual At-one-ment with the Maker of the body, God

The Blessed State, where the difference between the Maker and the user is abolished I call *Isvara Siddhi*. It is a non-dual Blissful Union or At-one-ment with God. It is the state of knowing whatever there is to be known or whatever you know *as it is*, *truly* without misknowing it, with impersonal goodwill and without personal likes and dislikes. That is the way God Knows.

Spiritual Progress

There is physical progress, financial progress, economic progress, intellectual progress, cultural progress etc. What is spiritual progress? Before attempting to answer this, we must first understand what spirit is. Before trying to understand a word, we need to understand how that word is used in a language: what meanings does it carry in every day use. I find that the word 'spirit' is used to mean three things: wine, ghosts or enthusiasm. It is also used to mean something, which is the exact antithesis of matter. Matter is tangible, but only with energy it is capable of causing motion, enthusiasm etc. Spirit indwells matter and causes it to undergo transformations. We experience ourselves as partly spiritual and partly material. To increase the proportion of spirit in our understanding of ourselves and, to reduce the proportion of matter in our understanding of ourselves is to make spiritual progress.

Ordinary men feel glad or miserable according to the extent of their possessions. Higher persons feel glad or miserable according to the excellence of their attributes. But wise men discover their true being, which is without or above attributes and they rejoice in that discovery. You are an *Isvara Putra*. You are a conscious being although you are deluded now. You are a reflection of God though you do not have that experience now. Discover your non-dual At-one-ment with Him. Be thou also wise.

Deepening of consciousness and increasing the taste of the bliss of your true identity is the direction in which you should seek your progress in meditation. After some time without your effort meditation will take its own course. Your *job* is only to begin it.

Right Awareness and Righteous Activities with *every* person that you have anything to do with, be it little or much, is the way that you should be moving. Let the new attitude transform the existing operative ones that will be desire and hate or a combination of both. If you have the basic attitude to serve God faithfully in creation, you will be liberated from the creation in the discovery of your true identity. God wants your heart. He is more pleased with heart without rules than with rules without heart. Encounter with every object and every moment of your breathing, as an opportunity for you to express your aspiration for attaining God and to become free from worldly trammels.

Key to Better Understand All Scriptures

I

God is playing a dramatic role as what you think you are - a mortal person qualified by a name, form, age, sex etc. He is playing so as to enable you to know what you really are - an offspring or son of God or *Isvara Putra*, belonging to Him and resembling Him. He requires your conscious cooperation to facilitate and expedite the fulfillment of His benign intention.

II

While all are offspring or son of God or *Isvara Putras,* cooperators are good offspring of God. Cooperators when they attain the realization of their true and God-like identity become true and perfect offspring of God.

III

To become a perfect offspring or son of God or *Isvara Putra* is tantamount to a rebirth in living, which will prevent rebirth after death.

The above is the key to better understand all Scriptures.

Muslim, Christians, Sikhs, Hindus, Jews, believers or non-believers are all offspring or sons of God or *Isvara Putra*s. All human beings are souls or *Isvara Putra*s including the worst sinners. *Isvara Putra* is what we all really are. This is not a label, but rather it is a revelation of man's inner and deeper constitution.

A new era in history is in the offing. This is the era of man's conscious cooperation with God, in both self-evolution and world-evolution.

I to You

Good offspring of God or *conscious Isvara Putras* are like brides of God engaged to be married to Him, waiting and endeavoring to qualify and equip themselves to be wedded to Him, in the greatest of experience called non-dual At-one-ment with God or *samadhi*. Thus, are they quite distinct from that large body of worshippers of God, whom I regard as flitters with Him, craving for various sundry benefits, not motivated by the deep desire to attain the experience of their non-dual At-one-ment with Him. I know that a large majority of people *at present* will not be inclined to take religion as seriously as I wish it to be done. But there is an inner conviction in me, that a time will come, and not in the too distant future, when there will be hardly anyone who is not proud to declare himself herself to be a good offspring of God or *conscious Isvara Putra* and live as one.

To realize that we are all offspring of God, and to live as loving sons, or daughters and faithful servers of God is the birthright of all of us. Nobody else's permission or intercession is required. You have only to understand, claim, and live what has been your heritage from the beginning of time. A better world, free from cruelty and brutality and the ruthless exploitation of others to further one's own selfish purposes, cannot come about by skillful legislation, a five year plan, or a twenty point program. It can only come about by more and more people electing to live as good sons or daughters of God.

Become a good son or daughter of God today, not tomorrow. Live as good offspring of God and live so infectiously, influencing others to live as you do. *The coming to be of a better world thus lies squarely in your hands, not in the hands of the government, or even in the hands of God.*

Will that not be a blessed family where the members live as good offspring of God regarding and loving others as good offspring of God? Will not that be a blessed place of work, where the members regard God as their invisible Boss and love Him, and love one another and serve Him, by all that they do? To love God, to serve Him by all that you do, and to accept His dispensations with a glad equanimity is your own innate essential nature, which is now dormant due to ignorance of your true identity. As you *practice* loving and serving God by your willed effort, the knowledge of your true identity or *swarupa gnana* will awaken and with that awakening, your true innate nature or *swadharma* will become easier. Ultimately, when your true identity is fully awakened, your innate nature will become fully bloomed, spontaneous, unwilled, effortless, and natural.

What I Want of You

I want all good offspring of God or conscious *Isvara Putras* not to be equally indifferent to all, but to be equally interested in all without any selective attachment.

I ask you to be anxious to live in a simple but definite way following the four spiritual practices as an expression of your life. Be not over anxious for wisdom concerning thoughtless awareness, ceasing to be a thinker etc. First be great soldiers of God. Learn to be great fighters for Him. Let devotion to God, love of humanity, *rasanic knowing*, and the concern for justice and righteousness radiate from your personality.

Do not be in a hurry for withdrawal. You are RA, the Unchanging Awareness, and you are going to know your true identity as RA and remain as RA forever. But it is rare to get a chance to be born as a person and serve God. So avail yourself of this opportunity and live like heroic good sons or daughters of God.

What I Suggest to You

A drop of lemon squeezed into one portion of a tank of milk will change all of the milk. I have not the least doubt that if you do what has been written above, the environment will undergo an ever widening and deepening transformation. The only caution is this. Gandhiji said, "I am willing that all winds of the other religions and philosophies, blow around me, but I will not allow them to sweep me off my feet." Similarly, revel in all philosophies and social movements that you like but do not lose the *simplicity*, *clarity* and *catholicity* of what has been written in this exposition.

We are all souls or *Isvara Putras*. We do not have to become *Isvara Putras*. We are *Isvara Putras*, whether we know it or not, like it or not, and accept it or not. We cannot cease to be *Isvara Putras* even if we want to. Even in our worldly life, there is nothing a son or daughter can do, whereby he ceases to be his father's son. It is open to him to be an unloving, disobedient son, but he cannot make himself cease to be his father's son. The father-son relationship is an irrevocable relationship, whether it is earthly or heavenly. Those who accept themselves as sons or daughters of God and want to live as good offspring of God can become a member of the *Association of Conscious Isvara Putras* and live in *God's Masqual Service*.

To become a perfect son of God, requires long and arduous spiritual practice. But to become a good son of

God, your willingness to become one is enough. I have written some thousands of pages, explaining a project for bringing about a better world to help you. Become a good offspring of God *today*, by understanding and accepting the *five truths* and working on the *four spiritual practices*, and play your part in the coming to be of a new culture where 'God's Will', will be done on earth, as it is in Heaven.

A
Prayer to God
(Fifteen Point Prayer)

Oh God! My Eternal Father! Ever present with me, as my Inner Ruler and Controller, *Antaryami*,

I am Your offspring, an *Isvara Putra*, belonging to You and resembling You.

I am now subject to beginning-less ignorance of my true identity.

To remove my ignorance, and to bestow upon me the experience of my non-dual At-one-ment with You,

You, wearing my body as Your mask
Are, playing a dramatic role as the person that I think I am.

My life is Your play, enacted through my free will.

I am now ignorant of my true identity and I am deluded regarding Your play.

Through my delusion regarding Your play, You are evolving me to attain the non-dual At-one-ment with You.

You require my cooperation by my becoming a conscious offspring of Yours, and by my practicing the four spiritual practices.

I am a good offspring of Yours now.

As my *sadhana* A

I shall practice being conscious of the truths about You and me, using the sacred words *Rader* and *Isvara Putra*, as the consummation of which practice I shall become a perfect son of Yours, knowing myself as not different from You.

And I shall practice being conscious of the truths about the life that I live, using the sacred words, *maskrader* and *maskrade*, as the consummation of which practice I shall become a witness of my ego, and my life.

Also I will be free from the delusion that I am a person, and free from all the suffering that accompanying it; and I will be free from delusion in the knowing of the world, and the suffering accompanying it.

As my *sadhana* B

I shall practice being conscious of the truths about You and others, using the sacred words *Rader* and *Isvara Putra*. At the consummation of this practice, I shall be established in the knowledge of the truths about others as offspring of Yours, *Isvara Putras* and of about You being their Inner Ruler and Controller, *Antaryami*.

And I shall practice being conscious of the truths about the lives they live using the sacred words *maskrader* and *maskrade*. At the consummation of this practice, I shall become established in the knowledge of the truths about others and the lives they live by and I will not misknow them due to ignorance and delusion.

Also I shall be freed from undesirable thoughts and suffering regarding them.

As my *sadhana* C

I shall practice to love You above all, be Your devotee and be Your conscious server in this world.

I shall practice to do and think all that I do and think in Your service and then offer those services also to You by reknowing them as Your play, enacted through my free will.

I shall practice to accept all that happens to me, whether favorable or unfavorable, according to my present understanding, as Your gift to me, according to the results of my past activities, for my ultimate good. I shall learn to remain in a State of equanimity in the experience of the vicissitudes of life, which are inevitable.

Also I shall practice to contemplate and meditate on You as my Inner Ruler and Controller who is just behind my knowing consciousness, and wait for Your Grace to remove my ignorance of my true identity.

As my *sadhana* D

I shall practice: to love others as I love myself, to treat them in righteousness in my thoughts, and to serve them in action as best as I can, not minding their adverse attitudes and activities.

And when the circumstances are favorable, I shall enlighten them of their true identity, and motivate them to cooperate with You, for the goal You intend for them which is the non-dual At-one-ment with You.